Playing the Odds

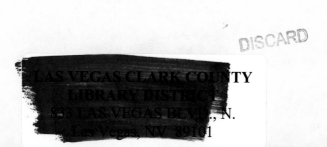

Hal Rothman in his backyard. Photo by Virgil Hancock III.

Playing the Odds

Las Vegas and the Modern West

HAL K. ROTHMAN

Edited by Lincoln Bramwell

Foreword by William deBuys

UNIVERSITY OF NEW MEXICO PRESS ■ ALBUQUERQUE

12 11 10 09 08 07   1 2 3 4 5 6 7

LIBRARY OF CONGRESS CATALOGING-IN-PUBLICATION DATA

Rothman, Hal, 1958–
Playing the odds : Las Vegas and the modern West / Hal K. Rothman ;
edited by Lincoln Bramwell ; foreword by William deBuys.

     p. cm.

     Includes index.

     ISBN-13: 978-0-8263-2112-1 (pbk. : alk. paper)

1. Las Vegas (Nev.)—Social conditions.

2. Las Vegas (Nev.)—Economic conditions.

3. Las Vegas (Nev.)—Politics and government.

4. West (U.S.)—Social conditions.

5. West (U.S.)—Economic conditions.

6. West (U.S.)—Politics and government.

I. Bramwell, Lincoln. II. Title.

     F849.L35R685 2007

     979.3'135—dc22

          2007013765

DESIGN AND COMPOSITION: *Mina Yamashita*

For Lauralee, Talia, and Brent,

the loves of my life, who share

the greatest of human characteristics,

genuine courage.

Contents

Part II. Las Vegas as Community

Part III. The Western Environment

Part IV. Looking Beyond Las Vegas's Borders

Foreword

FOR HAL ROTHMAN the practice of history was a contact sport. He would tell you that it thrives on push and pull, the competition of ideas, and the taking of stands. Its greatest eloquence demands frankness. Shyness and vacillation sap its strength, and no one who knew Rothman or read one of his many publications (least of all this one) would ever accuse him of either.

Like sport, history enlivens the rest of life, but unlike sport, its high place in modern society is compulsory, not elective. A sane and functional society—let's call it a civilization—must have a sense of history if it is to meet the challenges of survival and address the needs of its members. This is not because history repeats itself (it doesn't, so the saying goes, but sometimes it rhymes). It is because the stories of the human past teach us who we are and what we are doing on this lonely blue planet, and they find their repository in the annals of literature and history.

If history is so important, it follows that the arena of this contact sport should not be confined to the stadiums of academe. The game should be played in full view of the public, and the bigger the crowd the better. It should be played with honesty and passion, and the players, in addition to being rigorous and reliable, should be downright entertaining. That's how Hal Rothman played it, and, as this engaging and feisty volume attests, he set a high standard for anyone who would join him on the field.

The contents of this book consist mainly of commentary on current events, and to his commentary Rothman brings the well whetted tools of research, analysis, and judgment he used to advantage during an enormously productive career as a historian and public intellectual. The sixteen books (this one will be his seventeenth or eighteenth, depending on its timing), nine monographs, nearly two dozen scholarly articles, twelve book chapters, and score upon score of keynote speeches, conference papers, and mass media interviews attest to a personality that was rarely at a loss for words, that rarely, in fact, rested. For Hal Rothman the words have always flowed, but more like lava than water, glowing with urgency and sometimes posing a threat to the things in their path.

You feel that intensity in these essays. They pop with energy. Try this: "Nevada's emphasis on individual freedoms spawns a parochial selfishness that encourages people to think that the only interests that matter are their own." Nothing toned down there. Someone gets offended? So what, it's a contact sport. Or this: In Las Vegas "We make our living catering to the wide middle, planing the rough edges off of reality and spoon-feeding it to a public that hardly wants to be challenged." The tone is not angry, nor even chiding. It is brusquely factual. Rothman just calls it as he sees it. As he might say, "It is what it is."

His two principal themes are change and community. He urges us to look at change without blinking and recognize it for what is, not what we want it to be. The pastoral rural West of ranching and farming, for example, makes a poor model for the future. According to Rothman, that vision should be junked. Look at the facts without the blinders of nostalgia, he urges, and reallocate agricultural resources, especially water, to the cities and to the process of job creation. The West, after all, is the most urbanized region of the country. And speaking of water, the Colorado River Compact, he says, enslaves the Southwest to the priorities of a long-gone time and needs to be thrown out. And as for demography, English-only Anglos had better wake up: "The Las Vegas Valley will become a predominantly Spanish-speaking community." And so forth and so on.

Community is a subject even closer to his heart. The difficulty of creating it. The values needed to sustain it. The fragility of it. The absolute necessity of it for a life of meaning and value. Rothman, together with his wife Lauralee, knew whereof he spoke on this matter. Not long after they moved to Nevada in 1992, they helped lead the effort to establish the first synagogue in the Las Vegas bedroom community of Henderson. Religion was part of their motivation but not necessarily the greater part: they were committed to building community.

You would expect a writer as prolific as Rothman to have covered a wide range of topics, and indeed he has: national parks, fire-fighting, the American environmental movement, portraits of places and institutions, and more. But as a historian Rothman found his subject and as a writer he found his voice when he addressed himself to the shape-shifting, multiheaded phenomenon of modern tourism. Characteristically, he looked at it through the lens of community, asking how tourism changes a place, how it inevitably alters and frequently destroys the integrity of a community that hitches itself to the idea of attracting outsiders to come and "experience" it. Rothman had already immersed himself in this material when he and his family moved to Las Vegas, but once there he found every issue and every dynamic relating to tourism thrown into deeper and sharper relief. Las Vegas, urban avatar of the twenty-first century, became both his subject and his muse, and he became its leading interpreter.

He embraced the city with passion and energy, and in short order he grew into it and it grew into him like two vines on the same wall. Rothman belonged to the city, but he was not of it, for he was not a gambler, not flashy, not habitually on the make—although he would quickly point out that these characteristics are more the property of the city's mystique than of its permanent residents. He wrote of Las Vegas with affection but not adulation. As a historian with a broad reach, he grasped the city's place in the economic and social tapestry of the nation, and he saw it in the context of its time. No aspect of its life failed to attract his interest. Taxation, services, water, prostitution, politics, entertainment, real estate, even Elvis—they all merited his considered attention, for they all reveal some aspect of the city's truth, its underlying character, good and bad, the understanding of which is requisite for building a conscious and durable community.

Rothman always nurtured hope for Las Vegas. Without it, he could not and would not have devoted so much energy to its affairs. He hoped, in fact, that as a critic and commentator he might nudge the city toward a future that was healthier in all dimensions, more just and vigorous, better. He wrote so much and so often about Las Vegas because he wanted to help it reach "the next level." He also wrote about it so much because he knew no one else saw the city quite the way he did and he knew the way he saw it was original and true and that the story he assembled and that he unblinkingly delivered installment by installment, like a series of jabs, deserved—no, demanded—to be heard.

More contact.

I first met Hal Rothman in 1981 when he entered the graduate program in American Studies at the University of Texas in Austin, where I was already a student. He was then not long removed from his days as an undersized defensive back and kamikaze kick returner for the University of Illinois, nor from his brief career as a roadie wrestling amps, driving trucks, and fetching pizza for the likes of the Rolling Stones, Jackson Browne, the Eagles, and others—both vocations requiring extraordinary levels of testosterone, energy, and chutzpah. I remember him from those days as a kind of human unguided missile, likelier to collide with people and things, including ideas, than to go around them. He had curly hair, a weightlifter's body, and a wry, gaptoothed grin that broke across his face after each collision, as though to say, "Sorry. (But not really.)" The contact felt too good.

Years later, when I had settled in Santa Fe, Hal was a frequent visitor at my house. He was an itinerant scholar, chasing contracts and job interviews, and he was as intense as ever and nearly as reckless. Many academics channel their combativeness into passive aggression and endless disagreement over the pencil budget. Not Hal. He was fond of claiming that "he could pick a fight with himself alone in a telephone booth." I have never been quite sure of the correct interpretation of that boast, but if you heard him say it, you never doubted the sincerity of the wicked, just-try-me attitude it expressed. The young Hal Rothman was a walking, talking (always talking) bundle of dare. People who did not know him tended to give him a wide berth. So did a few who did know him, if they were shy about contact.

And so it came as a surprise to many, once Hal landed an assistant professorship at Wichita State University and the books began to flow, and he married and became a father twice over, that the still unguided missile that fired out from graduate school gradually metamorphosed into one of the leading voices in the fields of western United States and environmental history. The accumulation of responsibilities at home and at work seemed to confer a new calm and a new seriousness. Always generous in service to his colleagues and his profession, he became editor of *Environmental History Review* (later renamed *Environmental History*) and for six years gave it that rare kind of intellectual leadership that invigorates a young field and puts it on a forward arc.

Once he and Lauralee made their move to the desert, Hal also gradually became one of the most respected senior scholars at the University of Nevada–Las Vegas, an institution that embraced him as vigorously as he embraced it, and as the years passed he emerged as one of the pillars of his (adopted) home communities of Henderson and Las Vegas. The wild man had become a model citizen. The devil's fulltime advocate and arguer-just-for-the sake-of-it had become a go-to guy for steadiness, insight, and wisdom. He was still trenchant and forceful, not "mellowed" in the obituary sense of having given up the fight, but now he really knew which fight was his and where it lay. An enviable kind of confidence and peace seemed to come with knowing that.

In the spring of 2006 I asked Hal what he would talk about if he could give one more major speech. He said he would start by citing the famous campfire conversation near the end of *Easy Rider* in which Billy, the character played by Dennis Hopper, says to his buddy Wyatt (Peter Fonda), "We did it, man, we're rich, man. We're retired in Florida, mister!"

At this point in their journey Billy and Wyatt have nearly crossed the continent. They are somewhere east of New Orleans, far from the fat California drug deal that begins the movie, and seemingly in the clear. The viewer has to agree that with thick wads of cash hidden in the gas tank of one of their choppers they are rich beyond their dreams and that their past is unlikely to catch up with them. In their way, they seem to have *made it.*

But Wyatt, whom Billy also calls Captain America, fails to join in Billy's enthusiasm. Cryptically and quietly he says, "You know, Billy. We blew it."

To Billy this is a kind of blasphemy. He is dumfounded at his friend's desertion of their cause. "What?" he objects. "That's what it is all about, man. I mean, you go for the big money, and then you are free, you dig?"

His protests fail to move Wyatt, who stares wistfully into the fire and says again, deliberately, "We blew it." And then, "Good night, man." End of scene.

This line has been discussed and deconstructed a lot—by critics and by the filmmakers and actors themselves—and the consensus is essentially this: Captain America says, "We blew it" in the sense that Billy and he used their hard-won, individual freedom for no purpose greater than themselves—and all they had to show for it was money and a handsome pair of motorcycles.

As Rothman later put it in an email, "Individual liberation has turned out to be a heavy hammer on the [coffin] nails of community."

A few weeks later, timing his essay for the Fourth of July, he expanded on the problem of freedom-without-obligation in his weekly column for the *Las Vegas Sun*, wherein he called for creation of a Statue of Responsibility, ideally to be located on Alcatraz, a bookend to New York harbor's Statue of Liberty and a national reminder that rights and responsibilities, fairly understood, come bundled together and lose meaning when the connections between them are severed. "In a society in which people gave their obligations to community and nation the gravity they now only feel for their personal rights," he said, "they would participate instead of whine, they would vote rather than sit on the couch changing channels, and they would challenge what the media and the politicians put forward."

It was an excellent column, and it was pure Rothman: pithy, aggressive, and unambiguous. You will find it in this collection. But in an 800-word newspaper column you can only connect so many dots, and the story of how the hyper-individualism of the sixties separated from the communitarian idealism that was its birth twin and went on to become the neo-Spencerian "greed is good" doctrine of recent decades is a complex tale, laden with an abundance of dots that would take some considerable space and time to connect. It is more than a column, more like a lecture or a series of lectures, and I, like the rest of Rothman's many friends and admiring readers, would give a lot to hear Hal deliver it. But such an event is not to be. When Hal first brought up the subject of Captain America's delphic pronouncement, he was already confined to a wheelchair. Seven months earlier he had been diagnosed with amyotrophic lateral sclerosis, better known as Lou Gehrig's disease. Eight months later, the disease finished its implacable march through his body, and he was dead.

"It is what it is," Hal had said, back in June 2006, and as the days went by requiring more and more adjustments, more adaptations, he and Lauralee and their children Talia and Brent made them and carried on. Valiantly.

Hal composed many of the essays in this volume after he could no longer physically write them himself. His family and several dedicated graduate students helped him get his words to the page. But you would never know this from the essays. The tone is unchanged: forthright, to-the-point, absolutely clear-eyed. And always shrewdly and compassionately concerned (not a usual combination!) with how things are out in the world, amid the push and pull of the forces that produce what we will one day retrospectively call our history. These essays testify not just to Hal Rothman's penetrating understanding of the contemporary

American West. In their unyielding consistency and unspoken courage, they are also a testament to a life proudly lived, to the kind of moral stamina it takes to endure adversity. I don't know how he did it, but the weekly columns in the *Las Vegas Sun* kept on coming, each one fresh, insightful, and full of verve, long after anyone equipped with a normal work ethic would have abandoned the effort.

A while back I visited Hal. He was in his chair and his voice was still good and we could talk. I said I never would have expected it, but as I read the columns that he kept producing with clockwork regularity, I had finally realized that he had become a kind of city father in the Las Vegas community. His was one of the few credible voices that described the place, its aspirations, its values, and its true identity, to itself. How did he find his way to such a role?

"I have always tried to be a voice of reason," he said gravely.

"No you haven't," I said, recalling the unguided missile of decades before. "Admit it. It's a new role."

And then the famous grin spread across his face, gap-toothed and wry, as though to say, you caught me, but I won't be caught.

Reader, you are going to enjoy this collection of Rothmania, but as you read it, you may as well know that from time to time he is grinning the same way at you.

—William deBuys

Acknowledgments

THIS BOOK CAME TOGETHER through an unusual set of circumstances. My father, Neal Rothman, suggested that the columns I had been writing merited some kind of more enduring treatment. David Holtby was willing to see this collection as the fulfillment of an earlier obligation, and Lincoln Bramwell shepherded the project from its inception. Clark Whitehorn also brought his expertise and energy to bear, and Bill deBuys graciously consented to write the foreword.

Most of these pieces were written after ALS began to ravage my body. As I weakened, I learned to rely on a staff to accomplish even the most basic tasks. Two of my assistants, Leisl Carr and Jennifer Ward, translated my tortured speech into words on a page. For all their efforts, I am grateful.

Fun City, Las Vegas Boulevard. Photo by Virgil Hancock III.

Part I

LAS VEGAS as FIRST CITY
of the
TWENTY-FIRST CENTURY

Introduction

Creativity Las Vegas Style

THE HARDEST THING TO CONVEY about Las Vegas's ongoing economic success is the way in which its rhythms differ from the rest of the nation. Las Vegas is a postindustrial economic model, something new and novel in the United States.

Well, we are not alone in this transformation. Las Vegas's economic structure is fundamentally different from postindustrial models in other parts of the country. Even more, the people who analyze economies often judge us by the standards of industrial society, which leads everyone from filmmakers to financial writers to awkwardly stuff our figurative square pegs into their round holes.

The logic of our economy is different. The models for assessing it remained constant, derived from an earlier America, one in which manufacturing and agriculture predominated. In this new America of leisure and recreation, of service, Las Vegas has much to teach the rest of the country. Too often, our peers in other places simply can't see what we have to offer.

Richard Florida's idea of creative classes is one of the hot new ideas about how economies grow and thrive in postindustrial societies. Unfortunately, he too continues the ongoing trend of missing the mark about Las Vegas. Florida argues that to succeed as a city in the twenty-first century, a combination of culture, innovation, and high levels of education in the population is essential. This has become, in the colloquial shorthand of mass media, gays, grunge bands, and high tech. If you look at Silicon Valley, the Route 128 corridor near Boston, college towns around the country, and the exurban areas on the peripheries of major metropolitan areas, you can see how Florida derives his hypothesis. These kinds of communities share the traits that Florida values and they prosper.

Needless to say, by such measures, Las Vegas ranks low. Even though the newest statistics on college-educated as a percentage of the population show that we've reached and even exceeded the national norm, the kind of education, the Silicon Valley–type concentration of degrees and high-tech fields is simply not present here. Although Las Vegas is more open to gays than ever before and gay visitors are an identifiable sector of the market, we're hardly a mecca for gay culture. And the local music? Slaughter, a 1980s metal band, remains our greatest native contribution to rock music culture.

But we succeed—year after year. The growth since 9/11 has been spectacular, far more than could have been anticipated in the aftermath of that atrocity. The transformation of the market from room-based to a combination of room and residential units, and the continued expansion of the local housing market bode well, even if land values and housing prices continue to soar. So at least for us, there's something wrong with Richard Florida's formulation.

What Florida's model measures as predictors of economic success is really a cultural avant-garde, the creative energy that is typical of college towns and places where twentysomethings congregate. What he sees most clearly is the way in which the energy of towns like Bloomington, Indiana; Eugene, Oregon; and Boulder, Colorado, has moved to nearby cities like Indianapolis, Portland, and Denver, colonizing the inner city for single people and creating new and usually hip suburban districts.

This change does not stand alone; it is tied up with a decline in residential universities. As fewer people can afford college as a four-year hiatus, and residential colleges become more expensive and exclusive, urban universities provide growth opportunities. This has attracted start-up industries, which expand beyond the available resources in college towns and migrate to metropolitan areas, where there is greater opportunity for two-income couples and single-earner families, broader cultural amenities, and an opportunity to own better housing stock.

Indiana University–Purdue University Indianapolis now augments Indiana University and Purdue University; Portland State holds its own with the University of Oregon and Oregon State, and the combination of schools in the Denver metro area have begun to fill research functions driven by their location in a way that Boulder's aloofness from its surroundings does not permit. We're seeing the same thing in greater Las Vegas, with UNLV and its Shadow Lane campus, not to mention the William Boyd School of Law, now ranked in the top-eighty law schools nationwide, and the emergence of the School of Dental Medicine.

But Las Vegas is not an avant-garde town and never has been. We make our living catering to the wide middle, planing the rough edges off of reality and spoon-feeding it to a public that hardly wants to be challenged. It's been that way for a long time. Elvis's greatest successes here were after he was a middle-aged man, thick around the middle and jowly. He failed dismally in 1956 as a twenty-year-old, ripped and taut, full of the sensuality that repressed America would not easily allow. Only when he'd aged—as had his audience—and become a cliché of himself could he fill the showroom in the Las Vegas Hilton night and night again.

A few years ago, a group of Philadelphia architecture students came here and I showed them around. They bemoaned the lack of "culture" as they defined it. "Why do people come here?" one asked me. "I wouldn't come here if I got asked," he said through his white boy dreadlocks, in his shorts made from hemp, a ratty T-shirt and sandals completing the ensemble.

"You don't understand," I retorted. "We're not looking for you. There are plenty of hot young architects who want to be here, for whom the opportunity to design on a grand scale, in bold strokes, for a broad audience offers great excitement. They've got energy to burn, more commercial, perhaps, than yours, but creativity galore and they are challenged by what architecture in the future will look like."

The Strip is, after all, the largest investment of private money in public art anywhere in the world. And visitors treat it that way, as a vast sculpture garden. The young man had missed the point. He did not understand that commercial can be creative too.

In the end, what Florida and the culterati measure is only one kind of creativity. Their blindness to the popular culture market of the era of "me, me, me, now, now, now," the world of self-indulgence that has become the pinnacle of liberal consumerism, obscures their under-standing of us, and our absence from their formulaic measurement scales belies the reality of the importance of service economies in the postindustrial America. Until they can factor Las Vegas into the story of economic change, they can't begin to accurately describe the new reality of the twenty-first century.

August 1, 2005
Las Vegas Business Press

1

Gaming the Industry

WITH THE GLOWING NEWS of the opening of Wynn, Nevada's gaming win topping $1 billion in March, and the announcement that a new four-thousand-room Fontainebleau will grace the north end of the Strip, anyone could be forgiven giddiness about the prospect for another Mirage Phase, the eleven-year building boom that added more than sixty thousand hotel rooms to the city during the 1990s. This increase in gaming dollars and the move to build more hotel rooms belies the more complicated reality of Las Vegas today. Gaming's growing win is offset by its ongoing diminishment as part of the local mix, as we become more and more and more an entertainment destination that offers gaming rather than the other way around. Gaming is still the primary entrée on the Las Vegas menu; it's just that there are so many appetizers, side dishes, aperitifs, deserts, and after dinner drinks on what has become an enormous a la carte menu.

The tremendous energy surrounding real estate right now is seductive, but it might be misleading. It's been a brief but exciting merger and acquisition phase that looks to be ending. Partially this is a result of paucity of properties. What's left to acquire that's meaningful? MGM and Harrah's now control the Las Vegas market and while there are some choice morsels to be had, none of them are big enough to change the larger picture in a significant way. The real action will be in what I've long called the "beneath the radar" properties, the successful specialty niches such as Hard Rock and the Palms. The redoing of the Alexis Park as a gaming resort has some promise, especially with the big plans on the books for that part of the resort zone. But historically such properties have expanded the market, bringing new constituencies, rather than cannibalizing it.

Las Vegas has become an enormous niche market, not one market, but many. Despite the amazing success of the "what happens in Vegas, stays in Vegas" campaign, we cannot succeed by being any one thing. With one hundred and thirty thousand rooms, 83 percent of them filled nightly (a nearly insignificant decline in percentage since the 1990s that results not from diminishment of interest in the city, but from the pace at which the variety of supply is increasing), we must be all things to all people all of the time. We must continue to anticipate desire as well as reflect it.

Competition in this market is rarely head-to-head. One of the things that makes Las Vegas different is that staying at one resort does not—for lack of a better term—disqualify you from enjoying a direct competitor. As room rates rise and become more important in the mix—and there's nothing like the prospect of more rooms and more units to increase the pressure—competition between entities within the top sectors is a given. Three thousand new high-end rooms demand more visitors of a specific income level each night. Each previous opening in Las Vegas has expanded the market and there's no reason to think this one won't. What it may also do is change the dynamics in new ways.

Less obvious is the way increased average daily room rate (ADR) enhances competition not within sectors, but between them: why not stay at Monte Carlo and spend your time at Bellagio? Across the street from the Venetian and down the road from Wynn, Treasure Island looks like a bargain. All the experience at half the price! As the high-end becomes more crowded with new properties, but the amenities of that level remain available to all, the premium on the special experience—the status trophy so common among visitors—loses its imperative. It's not unique if everyone does it. Staying at a high-end property no longer serves as a trump card in the status battle of the water cooler. The experience that accompanies a stay at a high-end resort is more available to everyone, so inherently less exclusive, and becomes less worth paying for. If visitors make this choice, most often associated with saturated or declining tourist markets—which we are not—then the top tiers suffer and the wide middle benefits.

Added to that is the emergence of private residential possibilities (condos), and a shift in the market that enhances competition between sectors looks even more possible. If tiers two and three secure clients who used to stay at high-end properties and many other customers buy condo or time-share setups, especially frequent visitors who tire of paying high rates and would like to have some equity, this enhances competition in a way we haven't seen in a long while.

So in the end, the question boils down to the elasticity of the Las Vegas market. It has been and appears to remain as elastic as a market can be. The top tier requires such a high level of capital that entry is almost impossible to challenge if you're not already in it in some way. Its focus on expanding the reach to a wider share of the public opens great opportunities in the investment sector up to about $1 billion. It has historically been in that entrepreneurial realm where the new ideas get generated: Wynn and Glenn Schaeffer are the marvelous exceptions, high-enders who generate exciting new creativity. If the market remains elastic, then the competition seems most likely to be between rooms and condos; if it tightens up—if the new wave doesn't bring more visitors of that income level, a prospect that seems unlikely, then we'll see a much more competitive environment and probably a higher level of smaller scale mergers and acquisitions.

In the end, the hubbub is nothing new. It's the same level of economic growth we've seen through much of the recent past. We moved from the incredible growth of the Mirage Phase to a period of consolidation, when additions made more sense in most circumstances than developing new properties from scratch. Now new properties make sense; Wynn, Fontainebleau, the Stardust property, and others clamor for development. Residential projects from CityCenter and the Cosmopolitan to the fifty-acre Urban Village idea that proposes to extend the Strip to the south by its very advertising dot the local scene. We won't build another sixty thousand hotel rooms during this decade. We may well build a nearly equal number of hotels rooms and residential units. All tourist markets ultimately become real estate markets. The only question is what kind of market you'll be. We were on the way to becoming a retirement market; we may take a turn in quite another direction. From hotel room–based destination resort, we could move toward mirroring a ski town in our mix of offerings, a gigantic version to be sure, but a multitiered, mixed residential-hotel town nonetheless.

May 2005
Las Vegas Business Press

2

The Old Neighborhood is Gone

I'M A BIG FAN of the idea of New Urbanism, but I'm less thrilled with the prospects for implementation than most. To me there is a huge gap between ideal and reality in this case. While the idea that we will be able to live in communities in which architecture makes us more sociable is enticing and compelling, it also flies in the face of the really important changes of the last fifty years in the way in which Americans live, think, and act.

Higher density is coming to the Las Vegas Valley and coming fast. There's no doubt; the frenzy over what is widely thought to be an exhaustible base of developable land and the dramatic increase in housing prices has created an inexorable change in the physical shape of the local market. Condo projects are everywhere now, most directed at visitors. We're seeing some that are aimed at the diamond sheen of the valley, the people able to afford properties above $1 million. Condo conversions at the Lawrence of the market suggests the same phenomenon. At its most basic level, whatever the reason, we are going to live closer together and in greater proximity to one another.

But proximity does not inherently promote the community that is a singularly desirable element of the mythic America. The fact that people live close to one another, and in our case are likely to be atop one another, does not necessarily predict that they will return to the communality we collectively remember as an older pattern of American living. There are significant changes in the way in which Americans organize themselves, and these have a tremendous effect on historic patterns of community that so entice New Urbanists.

The first and most obvious change in the valley will be multifamily residences in a way that we've never before seen. If you look back over the past three decades, you see the change in single-family dwellings—first four to an acre, then six to an acre, now eight to an acre, and now multilayered dwellings, in some instances as many as seven to a floor. As in many more crowded countries, we will see a relationship between genuine affluence and single-family dwellings. The skyrocketing housing prices have outstripped the local economy. It's a question of time until single-family homeownership becomes a province of the well off. Multifamily dwellings are a form of cost containment at worst: at best, they provide a template for new patterns of living in the Las Vegas Valley.

But the leap from simple proximity to functioning community is incredibly large. So many factors mitigate against the conventional communities we remember. One of the key features of the way Las Vegas leads change in the nation is that transience is a staple here. The valley's population has quadrupled since 1980 and continues to grow at an astounding rate; the collective memory is overwhelmed with some regularity, requiring us to reinvent every aspect of community life on a daily basis.

This has a powerful effect on the way people develop relationships. Unlike the mythic America, where everyone knew their neighbors—an America that probably never existed—Las Vegans live in neighborhoods defined by affinity, not proximity. Your neighbors are the people with whom you share activities, the ones at your church or at your daughter's dance studio, not necessarily the ones who live next door.

Especially in new neighborhoods, affiliation is distinct from the America of memory. In that world, as little as two generations ago, we lived among people very much like ourselves. Almost everybody in the United States in those days hailed from a community of people much like themselves. It didn't make any difference if you were urban or rural, black or white, eastern European or western European. Your neighbors were much like you; you were probably related to most of them by blood or marriage.

Much of American fiction and local color stems from this world. You see it in the work of Sinclair Lewis and Sherwood Anderson, in that of any ethnic writer, and especially in the words of anyone who writes about their home place, southern, northern, or western. John Edgar Wideman, who writes of African American Pittsburgh, tells stories about community that are not different in the commonality that the people share from those of William Faulkner or Wallace Stegner. Richard Russo's *Empire Falls* has the same easy camaraderie of defined ethnicity; in Russell Banks's world, it is precisely that commonality that is the source of tension. Everybody's American stories were monochromatic, more about the relationships within a people than between them.

Such tight-knit community also fostered a set of relationships in the neighborhood. In that world, everybody knew you; your aunt saw whatever you did and reported it to your mother. It was no surprise. After all what you did, you did with your cousins. Word always got home before you did. As a result, a firm set of rules, defined by family and ethnicity held sway. They were clearly understood. It was easy to hang out on the front porch in that world, for you knew everybody up and down the street and were related to most of them anyway. And rarely, we remember, did strangers come by who were not of us. In short, it was a very safe world, one that did not challenge.

That began to change after 1945, when Americans moved from ethnic- and kinship-based neighborhoods to their occupational successors. Instead of living with all the other Italians, we lived with the other firemen; a few blocks over, all the policeman lived, at least figuratively. A few miles away, the white-collar workers clustered together, and the owners and bank presidents lived in an enclave around the country club, well before they would let anyone else in.

Yet that occupational world was different, for the taboos of the ethnic community first loosened and then disappeared. In the old ethnic community, someone might flirt with her sister's husband, but that was about as far as it went. Too many eyes could see and there was too much at stake. The taboos, the barriers of culture, the ways in which community shaped itself, usually roped in the most destructive tendencies. When people wouldn't follow the rules, those who exercised such desires typically had to leave the community.

The occupational communities had no such antidote to misbehavior. There were no taboos, no older relatives looking over the shoulder, no children of your intended partner in mischief who were also your relatives one way or another. Without the constraints of culture, the rules fell apart, and the divorce revolution followed with a vengeance. It has reached of course epic proportions, with one in two American marriages ending in divorce.

One consequence of the divorce revolution is the scarring it has left on the adults of today. A lot of them fear the kind of neighborly proximity that they grew up with. For some, it was the catalyst that broke up their family. Others have embraced the climate of fear that permeates our society, the idea that every authority figure and every stranger is a menace of some kind. The result is the remarkable level of control of children's lives that we see in our day and age, itself a factor that mitigates against neighborliness. Anyone who does not exercise that control is risking their child's safety.

All this adds up to a sad fact: living close to people is not necessarily a precursor of solid community relations. Las Vegas is incredibly cosmopolitan; we bring together people not only from all over the country, but from all over the world. The different styles often do not blend. Sometimes they clash, even dramatically.

The nineteenth-century political economist William Graham Sumner once observed that stateways cannot change folkways. We have to ask an important question in twenty-first-century Las Vegas: can architecture change folkways? Can we build community into proximity? Density, we will certainly get. Whether the community that advocates envision will follow is quite another story.

June 2005
Las Vegas Business Journal

3

The City's Economic Skyline

A FRIEND OF MINE who leans to the wicked once presented me with a riddle: what do Howard Hughes and Donald Trump have in common besides bad hair? His answer: neither ever built a thing in Las Vegas. Although that may be about to change as the city goes vertical, it's clear that what some have awkwardly labeled the "Manhattanization" of Las Vegas, mirrors Manhattan Island in other ways. Not only are we moving skyward, we are also increasing stratification of people by income even as we remove access to places long thought open to all.

What we're seeing wrapped into the redesign of the Las Vegas Strip as vertical space is also the transformation from the mass construction in the suburbs that has long sustained development to a new emphasis on elite urban living aimed not at families, but at the aging baby boomers. Let's face it folks, none of the projects currently being built on or around the Strip have anything to do with the local housing market. Most are either too small for local families to live in or are too expensive for the local wage market. A look up and down the Strip and around town shows lots of units in the $500,000 to $800,000 range with plenty more expensive, but infinitely fewer that are accessible to someone with the mean valley household income of about $58,000.

In this sense, the vertical living we've been promised, this new cityscape, is out of reach for most of the valley. As developers have rushed to get their name in lights, they've neglected the crucial features of the valley, our once stellar, long-standing, and now sullied reputation for attainable housing for the middle class.

The top end of the market is secure, both for the transfer payment part-time residents who bring us the gold that sustains us and for those who are sufficiently well-off to see the stunning rise in housing prices as an opportunity rather than a threat to their livelihood. There appears to be no shortage of such high-end living opportunities. The community is inundated with towers covering every dimension of the high-end market. The top includes places like Queensridge Place, a development slated for the Summerlin area with projected unit cost at about $2 million apiece. Every other niche down to the $500,000 mark is also crowded. Some even begin to approach overcrowded, as the smart money gives way to the knuckleheads who follow it as surely as day follows night.

But there's a rub for us in Las Vegas. The success of our city is two-pronged: it hinges on the glitz for certain, but even more, it depends on the service we give our visitors. All it takes is a trip to another resort to be reminded how well we do service here and how special it makes the experience. No one else does it as well; no matter what you pay somewhere else, you simply never get the quality.

The transformation of the real estate market and especially the growing emphasis on vertical development endangers that special feel. We've succeeded because the people who give service here could live middle-class lives, could aspire to own a home, save some money, educate their children, and someday comfortably retire. In this new market, with the ever-increasing emphasis on securing transfer payment dollars for new condos and other construction, the absence of new housing in the $150,000–$250,000 range suggests one more way that our paradise is becoming more like the stunningly expensive coasts. The gap between middle-class incomes and housing prices continues to grow, and there is no extant strategy to address it.

There's no way to sugarcoat this. As housing prices further exceed the local income scale, we risk the very thing that has made Las Vegas unique, the prospect of eternally good service. Workers who can live comfortably provide better visitor service than people scrambling to find a place to hang their hat in their own town. Every other resort can attest to this fact: when workers can't afford to live in proximity to their workplace, service suffers. In Colorado mountain towns, rising housing prices have forced workers to commute sixty miles each way over snow-packed icy roads to reach their visitors, who often stay in apartments converted to condos. It's hard to smile and be nice when you're worried about whether you'll make it home in one piece. And for us it's even worse. There is no hinterland out there and the cost to develop proximate satellite communities far outweighs the reward.

There's been some interest in creating attainable housing for the teachers we recruit, but really they are just the tip of the iceberg. Housing has become one of the most important structural problems facing the valley, a stone falling into a pond that is already creating ripple after ripple outward. The Las Vegas Valley needs a program to address this concern, perhaps a public-private partnership designed to protect one of our most important assets, the quality of life for the people who work here. The long-term consequences of ignoring this problem can be devastating.

September 15, 2005
Las Vegas Business Press

4

Western-style Gridlock

THERE IS NO MORE grueling aspect of life in the Las Vegas Valley than trying to get around.

We sit in traffic, offering each other the postmodern salute—you know which finger I'm talking about—and marvel at the stupidity and inconsideration of those who surround us.

We sit and we sit, burning genuinely expensive fossil fuels, polluting the air, and getting grumpier by the second.

Nothing is more demoralizing than the traffic jam. They've become commonplace here, a constant in daily life that we've surrendered to, forcing us to think of movement around the valley in uncomfortable ways.

Once, we said, nothing was more than fifteen minutes away. Now we calculate in forty-five-minute segments. Traffic grinds us down.

Surprisingly, we've actually done pretty well in our response. Traffic has gotten worse, but it hasn't gotten worse as fast as it could have.

Two major steps have been catalysts in slowing our bleeding.

Question 10, a measure for Clark County to tax itself to pay for transportation infrastructure, passed in November 1990. The initiative, spearheaded by Clark County Commissioner Bruce Woodbury, allowed the county to build the Las Vegas Beltway faster and farther than federal dollars alone would have allowed. No individual action showed greater commitment to the future of the valley than this measure.

The second catalyst, the effort to create east-west connections to facilitate crosstown traffic, has also made a significant difference. Since 1990—when planners referred to the Strip, the railroad tracks, and Interstate 15 as "the Great Wall of Las Vegas"—we have seen the construction of the Desert Inn arterial, flyovers from the interstate that have noticeably improved traffic flow, and the consistent opening of new roads and routes.

Nonetheless, we still see orange cones everywhere, still have too many one-open-lane slowdowns, and still sit longer every year.

Part of the problem is our strategy. No American city has ever built its way out of traffic, and we will not be the first. Roads draw cars like honey draws flies. Every new road that opens provides a brief respite, but soon enough everyone discovers it, and its pace slows to a crawl like everywhere else.

We're seeing at long last the beginning of creative solutions to our traffic dilemma. One is the growing interest in a comprehensive mass transit system.

We have an award-winning bus system, but it mostly brings low-wage workers to the suburbs, not suburban workers to their jobs.

The monorail provides a vision, but its impact on the city is minimal. It moves visitors. The great flaw of tourist towns is that they serve visitors ahead of residents, but in this case the monorail may have something to teach us.

Middle-class Americans don't ride buses much—they have the stigma of poverty, like trains in South America. But Americans do ride commuter trains, and the future of a commuter system, such as the one proposed by the Regional Transportation Commission (RTC), is bright.

Although every western city has been built for the car, rising gas prices and the inefficiency of our favorite mode of transportation, the SUV, project a future in which people will at least explore other modes of daily travel.

The old industrial railway from Henderson into the core of the valley offers a perfect beta test of whether mass transit will work here. If a commuter train can get people to work and back in no more time than a vehicle takes, then there's a chance of people buying in.

Another trend that bodes well is the change in how and where we work.

The resort corridor—along with nearby hospitals, the university, and other employers—creates the greatest concentration of workers and, consequently, of traffic in the valley.

If mass transit can serve this core employment district, it might be able to pay for itself.

Even more promising, much job growth in the valley is outside that central district. Each year a smaller percentage of the valley's workers are employed in that core.

More people work elsewhere and many don't commute; they live within a few miles of their workplace. Many of these people are self-employed, physicians and others, and have chosen this for convenience.

Many more, especially newcomers, have moved close to where they work. This pattern alleviates traffic congestion. These people simply don't participate in the morning rush hour.

While all the signs are hopeful, we still sit on the roads. We've been proactive, albeit in a conventional way.

This is a critical moment in transportation history in this valley. If we do nothing, traffic will certainly get worse.

The kind of innovation we saw fifteen years ago is necessary again, and it exists today in the form of proposals for a comprehensive mass transit system.

It may be that the best we can do is to slow the rate of increase of cars on the road. Mass transit has the best chance of achieving that small goal.

October 12, 2005
Las Vegas Sun

5

Senior Power

THE PACE OF GROWTH here has dulled our ability to see its effects on us.

Even though the cost of housing appears to be slowing the increase in population, we've added approximately seventy thousand people a year for the last fifteen years. This has provided consistent growth at a declining percentage rate as the Las Vegas Valley has grown larger.

We've done less well in figuring out who is coming here and assessing the impact of the needs of different constituencies on the community at large.

But there's an elephant in our living room, and we need to acknowledge it. The valley is fast approaching the dreaded peak-valley-peak population distribution, where a diminishing number of workers in the middle sustain a sizable young population and an equally large cohort of seniors.

It may come as a shock to many to realize that the valley is 25 percent retired and 25 percent Spanish-surnamed. Of course, they're not the same percentage.

Retirees are and remain overwhelmingly white, with a sprinkling of blacks that is substantial enough to have made Las Vegas the most integrated black-white city in the nation in the 2000 Census.

Las Vegas has become the first postintegration city in the United States, the first city to experience its growth after legal desegregation removed formal barriers to where people live. Statistical integration belies a far more complicated and less pleasant racial history.

Retirees who lived their working lives in the valley are still rare. In this we resemble Florida or Phoenix, places where people go to retire and where they build communities that are not part of the existing structure.

What we call "age-segregated living," a code for keeping children and teenagers out, follows. This kind of living is obviously appealing or so many people wouldn't do it, but it also isolates an enormous segment of the population from the issues that the valley faces.

Seniors in the United States are the best organized and most heavily represented group in the electoral process. They vote in great numbers and exert influence greater than their numbers on public policy.

The increase in the cost of living in Clark County has changed who the new retirees are. Unlike the middle-class retirees of a decade ago—a combination of Rust Belt workers, lower-middle-class southern Californians, federal employees, and those who had served in the military—we've seen a much more white-collar retirement community of late. Skyrocketing housing costs, coupled with the growing desirability of the valley, promises to increase its influence.

But the prominence of the new retirees sets up two potential dilemmas. The first stems from the tendency of retirees of all kinds to vote their interests, which is to say against anything that costs more than they pay right now.

Henderson experienced this in 2002 when voters by a 57 percent to 43 percent majority scuttled a plan to add as many as six new libraries. An owner of a $100,000 home, for example, would have seen his annual tax rate increase from about $18 a year to $32 under the plan. Voting against libraries within walking distance of your home? Seniors are the biggest consumers of library services.

As the population grays, it will become impossible over time for municipalities, counties, and states to raise money by referendum.

Seniors will vote their interests, and they will vote down, it appears, almost any kind of expenditure, even ones that serve their own needs, such as hospitals, police, and fire protection.

The schools show the other side of the equation. Already, children with Spanish surnames make up more than 40 percent of the population. In the lower grades the numbers are higher. This is the middle class of the future, the people whose prosperity will allow the workers of today to enjoy their own retirement.

Along with seniors, the needs of the young already strain the resources available. Both rightfully demand resources, but as their segments of the population grow, the people who pay most of the bills diminish as a percentage of the community. Where will the dollars come from?

We've seen the consequences of this volatile situation in Japan, where the stagnation that ruined the economic miracle of the rising sun coincided with the aging of the population.

Japan's economic growth has been stymied in the past decade as much by its need to care for its postwork population as by any other single factor.

The same thing is true in western Europe, where an aging population that receives marvelous social welfare benefits is set up over time to strangle economic productivity.

Despite the vitality of the local economy, this demographic issue poses a long-term threat. Growing populations of seniors and young people increase the pressure on the people in the middle at the same time the weak institutions of Nevada crumple in response to heightened demand.

This won't tear our ship in half and send it to the bottom in a heartbeat. Instead, we'll gradually take on water from little cracks and then larger ones until the weight of population finally sinks us.

October 15, 2005
Las Vegas Sun

6

Changes on Tap in the

"New Old West"

"WELCOME TO THE NEW OLD WEST" reads the sign outside Pahrump as you arrive from the west on the road from Death Valley Junction.

"New Old West" is a funny juxtaposition given the meaning of these two terms. The Old West has always meant open spaces, riding the range, cowboys and gunfire, freedom in the late-twentieth-century sense of the word—to do what you want, where you want, when you want, however you want, and with whomever you want—and a thorough and complete lack of regulation.

The New West means something different. Service and leisure have replaced extraction and animal raising, cities dominate, and people sit in traffic in SUVs, with glorious sunsets behind the nearby mountains that most never visit.

So what might the "New Old West" mean? Does it portend a rebirth of the nineteenth century, with gunfights in the streets like we presume happened in the Dodge Cities of that era? Or might it mean something more innovative, a place with the freedom of the Old West within the structure of the new?

Pahrump has been the butt of jokes for a long time. Portrayed as decidedly downscale, a little bit on the trashy side, and way behind the curve, Pahrump's growth to roughly forty thousand people and its aggressive plan to add ten thousand more homes spells the beginning of the transformation not only of the town, but also of its relationship with the Las Vegas Valley.

Pahrump is likely to become the next Henderson. Some people

once referred to Henderson, which is now Nevada's second-largest city, as "Hooterville." They looked down on Henderson for its industrial character, its working-class look, and what they perceived as its parochialism.

No more.

Henderson has become "a place to call home," the municipality with the highest household income in the valley, one of the most desirable locations around.

What drew people to Henderson, and started its boom in the 1980s, was affordable housing coupled with an opportunity to shape their own community. If you take a spin past the housing stock of the early 1980s, you'll quickly find that you're not looking at the Anthem of today. Most are small homes, 1,500–1,800 square feet, just the kind of places that ordinary people who work for a living found really desirable.

Henderson handled the first wave of spillover from the great and ongoing Las Vegas boom and it looks like this round will belong to Pahrump. Already, the outmigration over the hump is considerable and the growing cost of housing in the valley will accelerate the trend. Pahrump will become Las Vegas's first hinterland, whether the people there like it or not.

For a town that fancies itself "The New Old West," this offers a different future. If the patterns of the rest of the West hold true, Pahrump will find itself with dilemmas that parallel those of places such as Aspen, Colorado, in the 1960s and 1970s or Jackson, Wyoming, in the early 1990s.

Newcomers, people I call "neonatives," will arrive in droves, most fleeing the valley. They will be different than the people who live in Pahrump now, and they will try to re-create the type of community that makes them comfortable in their new homes.

They'll complain about the lack of services, the condition of the schools, the roads, the traffic, and just about everything else, failing to recognize that they themselves are contributing to the very problems they cite.

Old-timers, the people who came to Pahrump before this wave, will chafe at the way these newcomers are changing their town. "It used to be free here," some will mutter, "before . . . the subdivisions, the new casino, the last brothel," or whatever else.

Sometimes, this will just be grumbling. Equally often, it will be legitimate social critique of change.

All kinds of tension will soon follow. Neonatives and natives will struggle over local politics, and new subdivisions will elect representatives who reflect their interests. The town board will change.

There will be battles over services and how to pay for them, about what you can and can't do with your property—which you can read as a code for whether legalized prostitution can continue—and ultimately about what the community will feel like.

In the way that Henderson reinvented its identity, so will Pahrump. The Old West town will come to an end, but vestiges of it will remain. People will nod to that identity, and the further the town gets from it, the more precious it will become.

In the end, Pahrump will become another of greater Las Vegas's bedroom communities, the first outside the valley. For better or worse, it will take on traits of local neighborhoods at the expense of those of the Pahrump of today.

Of course, a lot of things will have to happen. Highway 160 will have to be expanded to handle the load and some kind of system to convey commuters will become essential.

Late to the western water derby, Pahrump will have to find its supply. But such issues notwithstanding, the "New Old West" will become a lot more like the New West. And once the hinterland begins, it will spawn its own clones.

October 30, 2005
Las Vegas Sun

7

Why No One Gets Las Vegas

THE BROADCAST of Stephen Ives's "Las Vegas: An Unconventional History," which ran last week on PBS, got me to wondering why it is that out-of-town filmmakers and journalists can't get Las Vegas right. An unconventional history? This film could have been made by the Travel Channel.

There isn't an original thought in it, and it repeats every hackneyed cliché about Las Vegas that has ever been uttered. How hard can it be to see Las Vegas on its own terms? Why can't they get it right?

Ives is a lesson in and of himself. He brought to the project an East Coast sensibility, which led it astray from the beginning. He and his staff never listened to a word anyone here had to say. In September at UNLV he introduced me to his friends as a senior consultant on the film, but as I told him and those around him, I'd rather be a Junior Mint.

The program was so bad it's almost funny. A bunch of people who don't know Las Vegas arrogantly serve as narrators; the people who really know something get bit parts. We are forced to endure the pompous film critic David Thomson and the smug architectural critic Paul Goldberger giving us our city's history.

Nicholas Pileggi repeats the same fictions told him by Lefty Rosenthal that make *Casino* such a good story but such bad history. The continuity narrator, Mark Cooper, looks like a stereotype of a Las Vegas lounge lizard; he gives us his personal outsider's view, the result of coming here since he was a child. Does he know anything about Las Vegas? Has he captured its essence? Hardly.

The film uses Cooper, a left-wing journalist, to tell Las Vegas's history, while excising excellent historians such as Michael Green, a history professor at the Community College of Southern Nevada, and reducing the eminent Eugene Moehring, a history professor at UNLV, to a secondary role. No wonder "An Unconventional History" is such a disappointment.

It's not only filmmakers. The *High Country News*, a respected regional western newspaper, recently ran a story about the Southern Nevada Water Authority and the efforts to negotiate water rights in rural Nevada. Fifteen years after the creation of SNWA, reporter Matt Jenkins still believes that "whiskey's for drinkin' and water's for fightin'," just like it was in the theoretical good old days.

Since 1991 the world of water has changed in mostly positive ways. Stakeholders now negotiate use instead of dumping water in the streets to preserve their claims. But a respected newspaper, or at least one I used to respect, missed that entirely and focused only on the potential for conflict.

Anyone with their heads screwed on straight well knows that groundwater is a side issue; the real battle is over the redistribution of the Colorado River. And here's a newspaper, the *High Country News*, that claims to cover the West.

So why can't they get it? What is it about us that is so hard for the outside world to grasp?

The first mistake is being unable to distinguish between myth and reality. Las Vegas is a city of illusion. It is designed to pull the wool over your eyes, to make you suspend disbelief, to pull you into the illusion so completely that you honestly believe it's true.

That's a remarkable feat and we do it incredibly well. We also catch journalists and filmmakers here like flies on flypaper.

The Las Vegas that people such as Ives visit is five miles long and eight blocks wide. It is not the city at all. It is a resort zone designed to provide you with anything you'll pay for. The rest of us live somewhere else and we are glad to show it to filmmakers and journalists. The problem is that they can't see the reality for the baggage they bring with them.

Even more, they lack the tools to understand a city devoted to service. Most bring the ideas and constraints of industrial culture to Las Vegas.

James Howard Kunstler, the former rock 'n' roll critic turned acerbic conservative architecture critic, spews venom at Las Vegas with every word. He thinks that we will be the first to suffer if energy prices rise so high that it is hard to move goods by truck. He forgets that in America, "if you got it, a truck brought it" is entirely true of his home of Saratoga Springs, New York, and everywhere else.

More likely, Las Vegas would pay higher rates for almost anything, and because visitors suspend their economic sense when they are here, we would likely pass on the cost. But what would compel a truck to bring something to Saratoga Springs? Because it always had?

Las Vegas remains a canvas for American neuroses. Visiting filmmakers and journalists come prepared to see the city and its people in a certain way, and in a place devoted to illusion, it is not hard to find what you came looking for. Often they suspend their best judgment when they get off the plane.

Some love us, others hate us, but all we do is reflect back on to them who they already are. No wonder they cannot get us right. They simply can't face their own reflection in the mirror.

November 20, 2005
Las Vegas Sun

8

Thoughts on the Newest City

in the New World

THE PARALLELS BETWEEN PRAGUE, the capital of the Czech Republic, and Las Vegas might only be apparent to me, but on a recent visit I was struck by the similarities between this wonderfully medieval city and our home, the first city of the twenty-first century.

Like Las Vegas, Prague's economy depends on tourism. Dominated by the Prague Castle, the Charles Bridge, and Wenceslas Square, Prague's core offers a fixed interpretation of a romantic past.

Called the "City of One Hundred Spires," Prague presents its religious and historic past now turned to commerce. Most nights there are a dozen or more classical music concerts in these fabulous medieval and Gothic churches. The acoustics are marvelous, but visitors couldn't tell the religious history of any of the churches, much less who was who in the Thirty Years War.

Every day Prague's workers stream to jobs in the center of the city, the core of the tourist economy. I watched Czech drivers sit in traffic, one to a car like American drivers.

Besides the cars with funny names and the narrow width of the roads, the only other difference I could detect was that nearly every Czech driver smoked. I never thought I'd see a place with a higher percentage of smokers than Las Vegas.

The stores in the core area were the same global chains we see almost everywhere. Specialty shops remained—Czech crystal still is highly prized—but mostly it was the United Colors of Benetton, the Gap, and every other chain store you can imagine.

The Czech Republic's marvelous history was intertwined with global commerce, much as our faux re-creation of Paris and Venice do.

Tourist languages dominated Prague's center, not surprisingly with English the dominant tongue. No one I engaged could not speak some English, no less than enough to complete a commercial transaction, offer instructions or directions, or, at worst, guide me to someone whose English was a little bit better.

American music and culture served as backdrops, teaching both language and culture. In a cab, the radio blared: "Don't you wish your girlfriend was hot like me." My Czech driver rocked all the way, singing along in broken English.

Prague even has its own specialty niche in tourism, mirroring the phenomenal number of niches in our economy. It has turned its old Jewish ghetto into the Jewish quarter, a seven-stop collection of synagogues, a cemetery, a community building, and the old town hall that collectively present a history of Czech Judaism and the Holocaust.

Despite its obvious draw to American Jews, always a lucrative tourist market, this story, replete with sixteenth-century structures, has strong international meaning. I saw tour groups speaking Japanese, Russian, French, Spanish, and Portuguese visiting the area.

Prague sells its past, with all its complexity and horror. Unlike Las Vegas, it is a fixed template, something that can be augmented with bells and whistles—concerts in churches and the like—but that relies on people's ongoing appreciation of both architecture and history.

The city also has a peculiar cachet, much like Las Vegas's iconographic position as the first city of leisure. Prague is one of the few major European cities not destroyed by bombing during World War II, so its medieval and early modern character remains intact.

The result is both a skyline and a series of structures in proximity to one another that feels truly old. The sensation is hard to replicate.

Prague sells its oldness, Las Vegas sells the new. On the surface, they couldn't be more different. But underneath, in the way commerce and attraction are combined, the way the part of the city designed for visitors is turned over to them, in the manner that people commute to that area to work but live their lives elsewhere, Prague and Las Vegas are strangely the same.

Tourism works its economic magic in different ways, but the structures that it sets up are much the same. Scratch any pair of tourist towns, look at the combination of infrastructure and people that underpin them, and they start to look alike.

That two places as different as Prague and Las Vegas would share so much tells us that the world is even smaller than we thought. It also implies that the future of the world economy is us traveling to Prague and giving them our money and them flying here and giving it back.

December 4, 2005
Las Vegas Sun

9

Bet on Las Vegas for

Western Solutions

LAS VEGAS IS A FUNNY PLACE to find solutions to the woes of western cities, but in southern Nevada, the phenomenal growth of the last twenty years has spawned innovative ways to solve the problems of western cities.

Las Vegas has all the problems of a healthy economy—growth, sprawl, air pollution, traffic congestion, changing demographics, inadequate public financing, and everything else you can imagine.

It's true that the remarkable changes of the past few years have transformed life in the Las Vegas Valley. The cost of living is 14 percent higher than the national average. Housing prices have risen in five years from the national norm to 38 percent above it. Homeownership has fallen below 60 percent, underneath the national average, and household income actually fell by $1,300 in the last twelve months, leaving Las Vegas below the national average for the first time in recent history. It is easy to think that the quality of life has gone to hell in a handbasket in a hurry.

The culprit, not surprisingly, is our incredible growth. Since 1980, greater Las Vegas has quadrupled in population. The boundaries extend farther every day, and people drive farther and longer in each succeeding year. The Las Vegas Valley is addicted to growth. Paradoxically, while growth doesn't pay for itself, growth foots the bill for what does get paid for in southern Nevada. Las Vegas has this wolf by the ears: it can't hang on and it can't let go.

Solutions come slowly. One good one is the Southern Nevada Public

Land Management Act of 1998, the best arrangement any American community has ever secured to mitigate the impact of federal action. It auctioned Bureau of Management land rather than allowing its piecemeal disposal, and targeted the proceeds for regional projects. Now, there's money for capital improvements, conservation initiatives, development of parks, trails, and natural areas in the county, and acquiring environmentally sensitive lands.

Another is a seventy-nine-species habitat conservation plan for Clark County that compels developers to pay a $550-per-acre development fee to maintain habitat for endangered species such as the desert tortoise. This creative usage of the Endangered Species Act was born of necessity, but it has become a linchpin in the development of wilderness and recreational space in southern Nevada. It also creates a convergence between the environmental community and developers, and nowhere else in the country has such a consensus been forged.

The world of water has changed and the Southern Nevada Water Authority should get much of the credit. This authority reinvented water in the Southwest, changing a nasty competitive situation, the famed "whiskey's for drinkin', water's for fightin'" of legend, to a cooperative model in which everyone sits at the table and people negotiate like grown-ups. This ended such travesties as communities spilling water into the streets to maintain their claim to their "share."

Las Vegas also developed a stunningly effective water-conservation program. Since 2003, the community has added more than one hundred and fifty thousand people, yet in 2005, the valley used 15 billion gallons of water less than it did in 2003. Las Vegas has saved one-sixth of Nevada's annual share of the Colorado River while adding a mid-sized city to its population. Can any other Southwestern city match that accomplishment?

Clark County has also built its own road, the 215 Beltway, around the city. When faced with federal funding that guaranteed that the much-needed artery would not be completed until 2020, county leaders acted. The result is a nearly complete beltway, built mostly with local moneys. Traffic congestion remains bad, but it would be a lot worse without 215.

But this is only a start. Las Vegas's growth-inspired problems continue to be legion. Air quality looms large. Even with the 215 Beltway, traffic congestion threatens to clog movement, and some form of mass transit is essential. Even more, emphasis on creating "live, work, play" communities needs to begin in earnest. Decentralization is as clear in Las Vegas as anywhere else, but converting to work situations that keep people close to home has yet to occur.

It's been forty years since the title of a book, *Learning from Las Vegas*, became a buzzword, and that book was about architecture. Now, western cities can learn from southern Nevada's successes and failures. It's time the region recognizes how much the future begins in Las Vegas.

December 12, 2005
High Country News

10

Growth Equals Worker Demand

A DEVELOPER FRIEND OF MINE was trying to hire a general contractor for a project. He talked to the man in September, and they agreed in principle to a price for his services.

When they spoke again in October, the contractor had doubled his fee. "What?!" the developer shouted. "Supply and demand," the contractor replied. "Be glad you can get me at all."

The year 2006 poses important challenges for the Las Vegas Valley, and near the front of the queue is labor. Our most unusual feature is the perennial labor shortage. We never have enough workers to fill the jobs available.

Nowhere else in America is ordinary work so highly prized. Nowhere else is labor as well compensated in comparison to the level of skill work that is required.

Economists have long regarded 5 percent unemployment as "full employment," when all who actively seek jobs have secured them. Except for the immediate aftermath of 9/11, Las Vegas has remained at or under 5 percent unemployment for most of the last decade.

This odd circumstance is a historical condition as well as a current one. It has been true since the construction of Hoover Dam.

The five thousand jobs at its peak were not enough for the additional thousands who flocked here to land a job at a time when one-quarter of the American work force did not have one. Many found their hopes dashed. The second largest expenditure during the mid-1930s in Las Vegas was the federal dole for those who could not get on at the dam.

The perennial shortage remains and we always need workers. And no wonder. Between January 1995 and January 2005, the valley added more than three hundred and fifty thousand jobs.

That's a lot of homes and mortgages, bank accounts, dinners out, and lessons for children. And that's also a lot of recruiting out of state to persuade people to come here and put down roots here.

But come they must if we are to sustain ourselves. Economic expansion in the valley is completely tied to growth.

Our entire way of life here depends on growth, on the expansion of the tourism industry, on construction and land development, and on the ongoing influx of people whose presence creates new jobs and other opportunities.

Everyone recognizes this issue, but only a few attempt to do anything about it. MGM Mirage recently sent recruiters to the Latino career fair, recognizing the largest local pool of potential workers, Latino high school kids who will enter the work force in the next couple years.

This is a sound strategy, but the larger problem remains. Locals alone cannot fill the jobs that will become available in the near future.

As 2006 dawns, the labor situation looks even tighter. The ever-growing economy creates new demands for skilled and semiskilled labor, demanding more teachers, architects, doctors, dentists, and pizza delivery people.

With an unemployment rate just below 4 percent in October, a full point below theoretical full employment, the prospect of finding a new pool of workers already living in the valley is pretty slim.

In the most simple terms, labor shortages drive up labor costs. Rising labor cost drives up the price of everything that uses labor. But finding that labor may prove more difficult than paying it.

With construction alone jumping from roughly 80,900 workers in March 2004 to 107,200 in October 2005, the pressure on the labor market will continue to be enormous.

And with housing prices still sky high, recruiting labor may prove problematic. Even for professionals, the cost of living here may serve as a deterrent.

Las Vegas has always been an opportunity stop. If people don't perceive opportunity here, they're less likely to come.

There are still guys who stand on D Street or even on suburban street corners waiting to be hired as day labor, but they are fewer in number. Demand exceeds supply even on the fringes.

We've got more work than we have labor right now. It's a paradox likely to get worse in the next twelve months. The need for labor will get more acute as we move into the next phase of growth.

We will continue to import labor, and it will remain a scarce commodity. If we can't get the labor, it will be harder to sustain the economic miracle that recent Las Vegas has been.

December 12, 2005
Las Vegas Sun

11

New Year's Eve

Cements Las Vegas's Stature

IT'S NOT REALLY THE NEW YEAR until midnight arrives in Las Vegas.

New Year's Eve is the triumphant moment in Las Vegas, the night we prove how far we have come. Every year, the party gets bigger; our status grows, challenging other cities that claim the evening as their own. We've long surpassed Los Angeles and other West Coast cities. Even New York now feels our hot breath on its figurative neck.

If there was any doubt, New Year's Eve shows how completely we have become a primary center of American and world leisure. As Las Vegas evolved from gambling to gaming to tourism to entertainment, we redefined the boundaries of leisure and gave it new meaning.

Las Vegas has become the first wonder of the postmodern world, one of the places that people must check off their list of places to see in a lifetime. Twenty years ago the idea that Las Vegas would be so central in American culture was preposterous, but the revolution we are in the middle of has catapulted us to an unimagined position of prominence.

First tentatively and now with confidence, Las Vegas has become the repository of American dreams. California has not yet fallen into the ocean, but it has lost its claim as the heartbeat of our aspirations.

Now that the Golden State is tarnished, people come here not only to shed their inhibitions as they always have, but also to reinvent themselves, to aspire to a future that might be out of reach elsewhere.

That the city is a mirror, which reflects their aspirations back upon them when they are willing to pay, bothers them not one bit.

When Americans think about leisure, they first think of Las Vegas. Nothing serves as more potent testimony to our success than the central position we hold in people's imagination. This year, more people will visit Las Vegas than Mecca—and no one has to come to Las Vegas.

The competitors don't really compare. Gaming elsewhere is really just a warm-up for us. Nobody ever went to Las Vegas, and after seeing the Strip, decided they really had to see Foxwoods. The best of the California Indian casinos still trumpet "Las Vegas–style" entertainment.

We dominate the convention market. Orlando, Florida, quivers as it seeks more public money to expand the very kinds of convention facilities that private money builds here. Our convention visitors have increased since 9/11; as of early 2005, Orlando's declined. Their officials concede that they chase the crumbs from our table.

Even Disney wobbles. It won't be long before football superstars answer the question: "What are you going to do now that you've won the Super Bowl?" by winking and saying, "What happens in Las Vegas, stays in Las Vegas—and that's where I'm headed!"

It's not only that we offer people the fantasy they choose, but it is also the deft way we shuffle the choices for them. In our enormous niche market, everybody's fantasy is available—for the right price.

You can take off your cowboy hat and become a rapper if you choose; just as easily, you can be nightclub elegant. Our special magic is the ability to change who we are—and simultaneously what visitors experience—at the drop of a hat.

So no wonder New Year's Eve has become our night. It's when people cut loose, what my restaurateur grandparents used to call "amateur night."

Everywhere, people pretend to be other than what they are, something they do nightly in Las Vegas. This phenomenon reaches its pinnacle on New Year's Eve, but our success is that here that feeling is not confined to one night.

Every night is New Year's Eve here; it's your birthday, too.

Las Vegas has always been a city of hope. It might be strange to think of "Lost Wages" in this way, but hope is at the core of what brings people here. They come with the faith that being here will renew them, will make them more than they were when they came.

So let's revel in the new year. The three hundred thousand or so people who were expected to rock our streets last night are part of confirming our place in a new cosmos. Being the first spectacle of the postmodern world has its advantages.

January 1, 2006
Las Vegas Sun

12

Immigration Demands Attention

ANY OLD TEXICAN would recognize the axiom "to populate is to govern." This was the principle of the Texas Revolution in the 1830s, that by creating facts on the ground in Spanish-speaking Catholic north Mexico, they would in fact establish an Anglo American, Protestant republic of their own.

I thought of this as I watched a Mexican guy, clearly an immigrant, cut sushi in a tony restaurant. He was wearing a Rising Sun bandanna, the emblem of Japan, and his knives flew. When I asked him where he was from, he told me "Zacatecas." Twenty-eight years old and a father of three, he had come to the United States like so many others to make his way in the world and do better for his family.

This is an old American story, one that dates to even before there was a United States. The *Mayflower* was filled with similar people, Englishmen who had gone to Holland to find religious freedom, only to be perplexed when their children came home speaking Dutch. It wasn't so much religious freedom they wanted; it was religious freedom in English.

It is this point on which the newest immigration to the United States hinges. As vigilantes patrol the border, they are trying to close the door long after everyone has gone. Recently, the national media trumpeted that North Carolina had the largest percentage increase in Latinos in the nation. Amid all the sturm und drang, few noticed that cities like Aurora, Illinois, had long been Latino strongholds. Wisconsin, that frozen white state—excuse the double entendre—has a significant and growing Latino population. Everywhere you look in America, everywhere work is done, you'll find Latinos.

One explanation for this change is simple: poverty, turmoil, and fear in Mexico and Latin America and the perception that the United States offers economic opportunity pushes people north. If western movies were made in Spanish, they might very well be called "*Norteño.*" They would certainly be about moving north.

Another is behavioral change. Since the two fastest ways to impoverish yourself in postmodern America are to accept all the credit card offers that appear in your mailbox and to have a lot of children, most Americans, more than two generations from the farm, cap their reproduction. There are exceptions, of course, but the birthrate of second and third generation Americans is nowhere near that of their immigrant ancestors. Nor does it match that of current immigrants.

Then there is the stickiest question, the cost of labor. American immigration policy is stringent on paper and lax in enforcement. We all benefit from underpriced labor, from workers in construction to the guy who cut my sushi that night. Immigrant labor not only fills jobs at the bottom of the socioeconomic spectrum that many Americans will not take; it also provides labor that allows prices to remain low. When *La Migra*, what Spanish-speaking workers call U.S. Customs, rounded up a bunch of Latino workers in Jackson, Wyoming, on Labor Day 1993, one hotel owner marched down to the police station and asked if the police chief intended to make the beds in his hotel.

NAFTA and CAFTA enshrine this arrangement on a wing and a prayer that such workers will stay home, but no one really believes they will. Agribusiness does not want these workers to stay home, and neither do you or I. Economically, we all benefit from their presence. It is fair to say that I could not afford my house if all the workers who built it had been paid the prevailing wage in my community.

So ultimately, it is the social issues attached to immigrant labor that vex us as a society. The spread of Latino labor brings with it a public dimension to Latino life that alienates some segments of white America. Latino labor puts children in schools, makes some demands on social services and law enforcement, and otherwise acts as any other community, immigrant or otherwise. The difference turns out to be who is asking for service or causing a ruckus.

The result is a kind of immigration that is surprisingly similar and at the same time different from the eastern European immigrants who came to this country between 1880 and 1920. On one hand, a group of people who seem foreign to the Americans of their day have landed in our midst. On the other, Latino culture is continuously replenished by its proximity to its lands of origination. People travel back and forth in a way not possible a century ago. Even more, they carry culture both ways, creating hybrids rather than the assimilation of the early twentieth century.

So not only in cities like Los Angeles and Miami, Houston and El Paso, can you live a life in Spanish and not be inconvenienced. It's true in Las Vegas, where the 85,000 Spanish-surnamed people in 1990 became 375,000 in 2004. It is equally true in large and small towns across the country. The Latinoization of the United States continues in earnest, often beyond the glare of all but the crime report on the five o'clock news.

As the influence of this community grows, the lack of attention from the rest of us may very well create an enormous divide that will someday come back to haunt us. In the recent chaos in France and Australia, we have seen how societies that fail to integrate minority populations pay for that shortcoming. The United States remains the best example of a polyglot nation; simply put, we bring all kinds of people under the tent better than anybody on earth. We're not perfect by any stretch of the imagination, but we still do a better job than anyone else.

March 1, 2006
Newwest.org

13

A Little Vegas in Everyone

LAST SUNDAY'S *New York Times* featured the classic tale of two cities: The paper sent two people to experience Las Vegas. One, Colin Harrison, an editor at Scribner's who is also a novelist, was given $1,000 for one day's lodging and entertainment. The other, Richard B. Woodward, who writes the armchair traveler column at the paper, received $250.

These effete New Yorkers stumbled over a crucial dimension of Las Vegas's success without realizing it.

Contrary to "What happens in Vegas, stays in Vegas," Las Vegas is never one market. With more than one hundred and thirty thousand rooms to fill nightly, we have to be all things to all people all the time. Our alchemy comes in many forms, but one of the most important is that no matter who you are, we have a niche for your taste.

You see it when you watch the people walk the Strip, looking at the modern city-states we have built, when you watch bettors play parlay cards in the sports book. You see it when the rodeo comes to town, when NASCAR is here, and on Cinco de Mayo. Everybody can be made comfortable here, can find their niche and feel like the town was built for them.

That's how we stay around 90 percent occupancy in an industry that would die to average 65 percent. All tourist towns reflect desire; that's how they draw you in. Only Las Vegas anticipates it as well, and draws from your choices what you'll want to see twelve months down the road. More than any other single attribute, this keeps us fresh and vital.

It doesn't take a genius to know that, with $1,000, Harrison had better options, but he sure could've used more imagination. A twentieth-floor room at Mandalay Bay makes sense, but with more than $700 to burn after paying for the night, he didn't have to resort to Las Vegas clichés such as Barry Manilow. "Zumanity" at least nods to the new, to more than nostalgia. But with all the choices available, for my money, he could've done more and had much more fun. Give me $1,000 and some space in the newspaper, and I promise you a better story.

Woodward had by far the most interesting time. There is something delicious about his writing, as if Woodward is self-consciously aware that he is slumming. After paying $142 for a room at the Flamingo, he was down to a hundred bucks for twenty-four hours. But what a twenty-four hours it was! Woodward and his running buddy, a friend named Chris, rented a Dodge Neon, and headed off to The Gun Store to shoot machine guns. On the way, they stopped at the Liberace Museum, entering late in the day and getting a discount on admission.

So far so good. Woodward was entirely consistent in the selection of activities for someone in the $250 bracket. The Flamingo, The Gun Store, and the Liberace Museum hit at the heart of America, where the average visitor from the average place would feel like they got more than their money's worth. The Dodge Neon was perfect. A Chevy might have even been better.

Then, Woodward began to count his pennies. He started looking for deals, free wine and cheese, art exhibits, and finally installation art. On $250 a day? Come on.

For most of America, $250 a day is plenty and The Gun Store is a legitimate attraction. The buffet is where they want to be and there is no shame in it. Most of America doesn't aspire to the avant-garde and installation art is well beyond its interest.

We understand that in Las Vegas and we provide opportunities in volume. Despite all the high-end rooms and attractions we've added in the last decade, Las Vegas maintains an enormous center. Truck drivers from Dubuque, Iowa, and hotel clerks from Flint, Michigan, can find things that attract them too. That's essential to our magic.

We plane the rough edges off of reality and give it to you as you would have it. Las Vegas does not challenge you. Instead it affirms who you are, an "I'm OK, you're OK" for the twenty-first century. Who you are and what you are is enough, we tell our visitors; pay us enough and we will make you into who you want to be. Even if $1,250 of the *New York Times*'s money mostly yielded clichés, it pointed out how well our niched marketplace works for Las Vegas.

March 26, 2006
Las Vegas Sun

14

Retirement Boom, Social Bust

REAL ESTATE AND RETIREMENT in the West will certainly become intertwined and even synonymous in the very near future, but the relationship has its drawbacks. The new "wilderburbs," as the historian Lincoln Bramwell calls them, will surely gray at a faster rate than the population at large. They offer everything the retiree of the future could want: beautiful vistas, trails to walk or mountain bike, small town, idyllic living, and plenty of enticements for the children to bring their grandkids for a visit.

What they don't have is a clear way to pay for the upkeep of services, to keep the streets clear and the water running, to protect the population with police and fire services and to pick up the garbage. Designed as something less than full-service communities, they lack the tax base and sometimes the critical mass of population to pay for services. Here will be the most difficult intersection of desire and reality: transfer payment retirees in communities in which their stake is short term.

Retirees fit the model of what my old friend Myles Rademan, Park City's "prophet of boom," calls CAVIES—citizens against virtually everything. CAVIES have an even greater impact than NIMBYs, the "not in my backyard" folks. They consistently vote down social services expenditures, even when they stand to benefit from them.

In places where these people have come to retire and do not have deep ties, their desire to take their rewards so far exceeds any feelings they have about the future of the community that they bend the wobbly steel structure that holds such communities together.

In their new homes, retirees are trenchant opponents of taxation in any form. They vote against everything, schools, roads, police and fire protection, and even libraries—of which senior citizens are the most frequent users. In Henderson, Nevada, a bedroom community outside Las Vegas, in 2000, a library bond issue that added $39 a year per $100,000 of real estate valuation when the average home was valued at $150,000 and would have built ten new libraries in a community that was roughly 40 percent senior was voted down by a 62 to 38 percent margin. Senior precincts voted overwhelmingly against having libraries closer to their homes. They preferred to drive, many easily spending the $39 that they would have been taxed in gasoline.

With such behavior, retirees present a dilemma. They take more out of the system than they put in, and like everyone else, they don't rush forward to offer more than their share. Even more, their heavy weight in communities and their consistent presence at the polls sit down on the rest of the community, preventing other constituencies from achieving their ends. To frustrated families with children or civic-minded individuals, the interests of retirees seem parochial and self-centered.

Retirees provide an economic boost to the communities they enter, but it comes at a cost. Job creation is a certainty, but the nature of the jobs is often in question. Retirees require an entire range of services, only a few of which require high levels of skill.

When workers come, some tend to stay. Retirement communities become havens for unskilled workers, landscape gardeners and yard men, gurney pushers and orderlies, and restaurant workers and street cleaners. These people bring their families to the same communities and put down roots. That work force is, of course, at least partially immigrant, often not fluent in English. Communities that embrace retirees can expect a lot of low-wage labor and that means growing populations of people who earn low wages and often need social services. This leads to a need for more revenue to provide more services, exactly what retirees vote down at the polls, time and again.

The people who wind up footing the bill are—no surprise—those in their working years, between the ages of eighteen and sixty-five.

Increasingly, they are the sandwich generation, caught between aging parents and the children they are raising. Communities depend on their labor, and indeed their civic involvement, to make a place home.

Trapped between two different kinds of open mouths, children and seniors, the latter always loudly asserting that they have earned a pass on financial obligations to the community, the sandwich generation already views seniors with the disdain of a society that would readily eat its old. Both seniors and the young drain the public till. The only place to get more resources is the working population. The seniors are too well organized and the young do not earn enough.

Regressive tax structures throughout the West and the demands of vocal constituencies who don't pay their way complicate local decision making. All the economic benefit in the world from retirement won't diminish this conflict.

In the communities of the future, large numbers of children and large numbers of retirees will become common. For anyone in their working years, this is a disastrous formula, the dreaded peak-valley-peak demographic curve. Unfortunately, the valley is in the middle, filled with people in their prime years of work who pay most of a society's bills. As this cohort makes up a smaller percentage of the American work force, we risk the stagnation that has already encompassed Japan and is turning Europe into a Muslim continent.

Japan did not cease its economic growth because of a lack of ingenuity. Instead, it was weighed down by its low birthrate and increasing life spans, both dilemmas that we offset with immigrant labor, legal and *sin papeles*, "without papers," as such workers refer to themselves.

The contours of this future are already apparent in the Las Vegas Valley, but it offers a hardly pleasant vision of the future. In 2005, 25 percent of the more than 1.8 million in greater Las Vegas were retired; another 25 percent were Latino. Needless to say, the two groups barely overlapped.

Most of the retirees walking the trails of the neighborhoods in the morning, going to coffee shops, attending movies, gambling in casinos, and babysitting their grandkids are white. A growing percentage of younger workers, especially unskilled workers, were not. More and more, the faces of the work force were becoming brown, yellow, and black. In the palette of colors, this future looked uncomfortable, one color served, many more serving.

It may be that the future of this country is older, more affluent white people who experienced opportunity in their working lives served by younger, less affluent nonwhites with a smaller chance to achieve the standard of living of the people they care for. Throughout the nation, as the primary beneficiaries of the stock market run-up of the 1990s and the surge in federal spending since 2000 gray, they will increasingly depend on nonwhites to provide their care. In situations where the care-providers see no future, perceive a grind of poorly paid and unappreciated service for cranky old people, another kind of tear at the fabric of social civility is certain.

April 10, 2006
Newwest.org

15

The Mall of America

Has Nothing on Vegas

THERE IS NOTHING LIKE TRAVELING to other places to remind us how well Las Vegas performs its magic and how much the rest of the world still has to learn from us. During a recent trip to Minnesota, I visited the Mall of America, the self-proclaimed "biggest shopping center in the world." But a quick cruise around one portion of the mall and I was ready to go.

Nothing special there. The shops were ordinary; the entertainment flat, a bad county fair. Even the prospect of an array of Elvis impersonators the next day could not get me back. It was not even up to the standards of Circus Circus. Once again, Las Vegas's attractions trump all others. What do you expect in a town where A-entertainment goes begging?

The Mall of America opened in 1992, the same year as the Forum Shops at Caesars. Billed as the greatest shopping experience on Earth, the mall has miles of shopping, more than even the most self-indulgent American—a believer in the idea that being American means that anything worth doing is worth overdoing—could manage.

In design, there is nothing fancy about the Mall of America. It simply melded the American penchant for size with a common feature of cold northern cities, the connected downtowns of places such as Minneapolis and Spokane, Washington. In these frozen cities, you can access almost any part of the downtown by connected walkways. This way, you go from your attached garage to your indoor parking and then to your office without ever going outside. Even better, you can go out to lunch, shop, and fill every other need, never encountering the always dreary and freezing cold.

The Mall of America simply took this idea and reversed its direction. Instead of linking downtown by connective walkways, it built an enormous downtown as a shopping experience, well away from the downtown of either of the Twin Cities.

With four floors of shopping and four anchor tenants, everything you need for a consumerfest was there. One of my companions, a known shoe horse, was ecstatic that he could visit the biggest Nordstrom in the world. He was sure he would find a couple of pairs of Italian shoes that he could not find anywhere else. After all, bigger is better, right?

If raw consumption is what you are after, this idea works. I would venture that any store in any mall in America is replicated in the Mall of America. But that is where the imagination ends and Las Vegas begins.

The Forum Shops have been reborn time and again since 1992. The statues move; they speak. The sky changes. There is a kind of life to the place, a sense of self that is much more than simply consumption. It entertains your spirit, even your mind, as well as lightening your wallet more than a little.

And the Forum Shops are the oldest and strangely most stolid of Las Vegas's shopping attractions. Since they opened, we have undergone a remarkable transformation in retail amenities. It is no longer enough to simply sell something on the Las Vegas Strip. You have to entertain along with it.

So we see the shopping at each of the hotels, the redesign of the Fashion Show mall, each with its set of tricks that draws you into its theme. You are never just shopping in Las Vegas. You are always making yourself into something new.

Rather than waste my money, I am going to go back to vacationing on the Strip. Not only do I save the airfare, but I also see more of the world—at least as portrayed by Las Vegas hoteliers—and I get better experience for my buck. Entertainment and shopping have become the same thing. It is no longer about the goods, but about the way you acquire them.

So even though the Mall of America claims 35 million to 40 million visits a year, comparable to the number of visitors to Las Vegas, our ability to sustain illusion provides an emotionally more fulfilling experience than the grandiose, oversized shopping of the Mall of America. It is hard to call Las Vegas subtle, but in comparison, we are quite refined.

April 16, 2006
Las Vegas Sun

16

Cool Market, High Prices

I PULLED MY HAND BACK from the hot griddle that has been Las Vegas residential real estate and found to my surprise for the first time in a couple of years, my hand was not scorched.

What a difference two years makes. In 2004 the market was as hot as could be imagined. Last year condo towers were the talk of the day. Even those have now fallen by the wayside, closed down or in court, victims of the greatest of Las Vegas truisms: no place makes people's eyes bigger than their stomachs more than Las Vegas does.

But now we find that the residential market has been turned upside down. Once scarcity was the watchword; now we have a glut of properties, more than fifteen thousand at last glance, and the beginning of the employment sector's softening. Everyone is talking about unemployed real estate agents, mortgage brokers, and appraisers. Twelve months ago people flocked to these occupations in search of easy riches.

Since the residential market shot up in 2003, many homes here have been out of reach for local buyers. Simply put, the average local income did not allow the purchase of the average house, even with all the bells and whistles that characterize residential lending in Las Vegas. So who is buying all these houses and why are they all of a sudden less interested?

The Las Vegas residential market has been driven by transfer payment dollars, money earned elsewhere and brought here, presumably because it bought more here than wherever it was made. Outside dollars set prices here. The local wage scale had little to do with the cost of housing.

This is more than a tortured explanation for California colonialism. For a long time, such a pattern was the clearest feature of the Las Vegas Valley. Blue-collar Californians could find considerably better value for their dollar here; many cashed out a 1,200-square-foot home in California for $400,000 and came here and bought twice the house at half the price. But that was before the boom.

Since then, we have been caught in a conundrum. Las Vegas was an ideal destination when our housing prices were less than 80 percent of the cost in southern California. During the last two years, we have pushed that line, making a move to southern Nevada more personal choice than mandatory economic decision. For blue-collar workers and retirees, Las Vegas is much less of an option than ever before. Pahrump and the other new hinterland communities are more to their economic liking, if they are going to move at all.

So who is coming? Clearly, it is a more affluent group. A quick look at housing prices proves that. With new homes in tony suburbs beginning in the $500,000 range, there are very few first-time owners rushing to buy. Instead, we have grafted an upper middle class onto the valley, older than the average and looking for the amenities we provide.

All their money is not earned here, but it spends very well. The houses get bigger and more luxurious and the roads are clogged with more and more high-end vehicles. It is a salesman's paradise: affluent consumers everywhere.

So despite the cooling of the market, do not expect real estate prices to return to the halcyon days of the late 1990s. Too much outside money is lined up, seeking to move here and often retire here. These dollars will hold up the market, allowing softness but keeping prices relatively stable.

This is good if you are already a homeowner. You will very likely get to keep a good portion of the paper profit of recent years. That makes the home equity loan you took out to buy that boat a pretty good bet.

If you are looking to get into home ownership for the first time, the news is not as good. The bottom of the market is going to remain pretty high, maybe even out of reach. The days of a 3 to 1 ratio between the average home price and the average wage are gone forever.

For a long time, Las Vegas had coastal amenities and Midwestern prices. That was an important part of our allure. Now we have coastal amenities and prices that are darn close to the coast. It did not take an earthquake to give Las Vegas beachfront property—at least in cost.

June 4, 2006
Las Vegas Sun

17

Clean Air Act Pits the

State's Tradition v. Its Future

I HAVE ALWAYS thought of myself as a liberal on the issue of smoking. It only seems fair that people could smoke wherever they wanted—as long as they held all the smoke in their lungs. That way, people who need their nicotine could have it and I, along with all the other non-smokers in the world, would not have to smell tobacco.

But, of course, the world is more complicated. Stand under any overhang at the edge of any building that forbids smoking and you find the smokers' enclave. Clustered in clumps, smokers enjoy their almost-forbidden pleasure, leaving the distinct aroma of their presence after they finish. I for one instinctively flinch and hold my nose as I approach such places, knowing full well that the smell of stale tobacco will soon hit me in the face.

Casinos are different. They allow smoking, the best of them pulling the smoke from the air as if by magic. Even though people are smoking around you, you never smell it unless you are in the immediate vicinity of a lit cigarette. The next day, when you sniff your clothes, you can always smell the smoke, but while you are there, the world seems smoke-free.

The prevalence of smoking is part of being in Nevada, the nation's closest thing to a libertarian state. We have always allowed more here, first as economic necessity and then as habit. In Nevada, you remain free in the late-twentieth-century version of the term: you can do what you want, where you want, how you want, and with whomever you want. Paul Revere might not recognize this as freedom, but generations of Nevadans have.

That may be about to change. The Nevada Indoor Clean Air Act proposes to make it illegal to smoke in restaurants, bars, and other places that serve food. Casinos are exempted. This is a first in Nevada, an effort to regulate personal behavior that is not illegal. Modeled on a counterpart measure in California, the legislation would fundamentally change the way we do business in the Silver State.

Smoke-free works. California's bars and restaurants are a pleasure. You can sit for hours, never getting a whiff of tobacco—until you leave the building and find the smokers crowded under the overhang. On a certain level, we trade a smoke-free indoors for a smoke-filled outdoors.

A recent judicial ruling expands the range of the Nevada Indoor Clean Air Act, however, to include hotel and motel rooms as places where smoking is forbidden. If anything guarantees the failure of this measure at the polls, it is this ruling. It goes too far from the basic default of what Nevada means to persuade the voters. While we may be willing to regulate the spaces in which the public socializes, we are not yet ready to regulate a transaction between a willing lessor and a willing tenant.

But the measure and the court ruling are a portent of things to come. The state has changed, and the old Nevada is outnumbered by the new, by a ratio of somewhere between 5 and 7 to 1. So many people have moved here that they have been like a huge wave on a sand castle. You can see the outline of what was, but the clear picture of what it was is obscured.

A new Nevada is constantly forming, and its values are shaped in other places and translated here. There is much of the old anti-institutional vision in newcomers, but even more of them are suburban with the expectations of suburbanites. Retirees present another version of the new Nevada, as do Hispanics.

I fully expect the Nevada Indoor Clean Air Act to fail, in no small part because of the ruling this past week. It might make sense to the public to make bars and restaurants smoke-free, but hotel and motel rooms offer a different vision that I doubt Nevadans will embrace.

Pass or fail, such legislation will continue to come. Nevada has changed, and the old core who self-selected for an institution-free life in the Silver State is now a minority in its own paradise.

Even more, Nevada's traditions and its future are on a collision course, with the demands of the new Nevada, sometimes for government service, other times for regulation of behavior like smoking and nude dancing, at odds with the way things have always been done here. How we work out this particular tension will tell a great deal about the future of the Silver State.

June 11, 2006
Las Vegas Sun

18

How Las Vegas Growth Shaped

the American Downtown

I STOOD NEAR the new South Coast project, admiring the sleek lines of its architecture and thinking about the ways such developments seed a different future than previous generations of urban Americans ever envisioned. It promises a future that we see all over the Las Vegas Valley, one that is already common across the nation, but also can be seen in crystal clear high relief here.

Cities of the Industrial Age had vital core areas that drove their economies. They had magnificent public and private buildings, museums like the Museum of Modern Art in New York or the Field Museum in Chicago, to attest to their prominence. Huge factories and office buildings clustered around these magnificent edifices. Often you could smell the industry as you walked into the museum or the performing arts center; but all understood that the smell was that of prosperity, of wealth, of local success.

Las Vegas was different. We never had that kind of center. Our "downtown" was where the train stopped, a creation of the land auction that we celebrated the hundredth anniversary of last year. More reminiscent of American towns than cities, it was only barely a downtown, a captive of the changing ways Americans moved. When we traveled by train, that was our center.

When we first traveled by car, the Strip became our downtown. It was different than most American downtowns, where you could shoot off a cannon after 5:00 p.m. and never hit anybody. For a long time, locals used the Strip as their playground. In those long-lost halcyon days, there was a shoulder season here; we actually got the town back from its visitors once in a while. And then we knowingly played in their playground.

The great growth spurt that began in the late 1980s and continues to this day did something remarkable: it destroyed whatever core of a city we had and made us into many cities. It is not only Boulder City, North Las Vegas, Henderson, and the city of Las Vegas, the formal jurisdictions besides Clark County in the valley. We have further devolved into neighborhood-based communities like the South Coast that perfectly illustrate the future.

Essentially, the physical center here did not hold. Las Vegas once meant the area on both sides of Interstate 15 from downtown to roughly Tropicana. Beyond that was way out there. That community had institutions that served it, clubs and bowling alleys, restaurants and libraries, churches and synagogues. But the constant pressure of more newcomers every year taxed those institutions, for the demand upon them was far greater than they had been designed to bear.

The result was the fracturing of one "city" into many. Everywhere you see a Station or Coast casino, you have a small city that revolves around the hotel-casino-movie theaters-restaurants at its core. Sam's Town was the first; the nine primary Station properties all qualify as community centers, as do five of the Boyd-Coast properties. That is at least fourteen cities in the valley.

Two changes contributed to this new reality. The institutions of the pre-1985 Las Vegas Valley were not strong enough to withstand the growth. The neighborhood casinos stepped into the vacuum, offering all the features anyone could want. It became natural to seek in private space what had once been the province of downtown: a movie, a stroll afterward with an ice cream cone, and with the added advantage that you could play a few slots if you chose.

The people who came to the new suburbs were different than the people who had been here before. In 1980 almost everyone who was retired here had lived their working life in the valley. That is so far from true today that it defies comprehension. Retirees come here from all over the country, outnumbering local retirees by an exponential ratio. The newcomers lacked any ties to the region and the all-in-one experience of the casino/entertainment center was appealing. Instead of driving from strip mall to strip mall, they could have it all at one stop.

Such people have no ties to downtown Las Vegas or even the Strip. They live in their neighborhood, defined not by municipality or income bracket, but by where they go for dinner and fun on Saturday night. They have created many cities out of the one we once were, replacing community-wide institutions with neighborhood ones. Casinos, malls, and airports became the same places a while ago; people have embraced this vision of life here. The urban future is already here.

July 9, 2006
Las Vegas Sun

19

The Old-Fashioned Approach to Growth

THE MANHATTANIZATION OF LAS VEGAS is over. This gassy phrase captivated the regional imagination, but it turns out to be more smoke than substance.

We are not going to see a skyline that resembles the urban spaces of New York. Nor are we going to become a city of pedestrians who use public transportation to get where we are going. The idea was over-blown to begin with; the phrasing was typical Las Vegas, designed to appeal to people whose eyes are bigger than their stomachs.

When the condo boom began almost two years ago, it was clear to anyone with any sense that most of the projects were conceived on a wing and a prayer, but I do not think anyone expected such a complete fiasco. A number of factors intervened.

The single biggest problem was that too many people without experience in this complicated market discovered it at the same time. Simply put, there were too many projects that were too similar, both in amenities and price. The proposed towers all looked the same, and their pitchmen sounded the same. Who could tell them apart? And why would they bother?

Even more, the price on most of the units was above $400,000, well outside the range of most Las Vegas families. This meant that the entire market was designed to appeal to the investor class, people for whom having a condo in Las Vegas was a desirable write-off of one kind or another. Such people are savvy; they have money and know how to use it to their advantage. Typically skilled at investing, they knew junk when they saw it.

Another intangible became the growing shortage of materials. It has become fashionable to blame this on Hurricane Katrina, but in reality, it is a symptom of a larger global problem over the competition for resources.

The expansion of China's economy has put tremendous pressure on raw materials. With a 10 percent growth rate, China sucks up almost every loose piece of steel or yard of cement. That meant Las Vegas builders were paying higher prices for materials even before the local demand soared. That drove up already exorbitant costs and prices followed.

Nor was there enough skilled labor in the Las Vegas Valley for all these projects. We have always had a shortage of labor here, but never before has it been so severe. Las Vegas contractors have been having a field day. One fellow I know tells of a general contractor who gave him a price one month and then asked for double the next. When the man balked, the contractor said that he was welcome to find someone else. Of course, there was no one else available.

This extends all the way through the skilled trades, the plumbers and electricians. There has always been a premium on skill in greater Las Vegas, but it has never been as acute as it is now. Everyone with trade skills is booked halfway into the 2010s.

What this means is what it has always meant—a rush to dependable brands and projects where the quality is guaranteed and the work will get done. In the newest Las Vegas, the post-Mirage Phase market in which we live, this means MGM Mirage. The company that staked its future with the Las Vegas Valley has become the largest real estate developer in Nevada history. Its bricks-and-mortar operations inspire confidence in buyers. They are lining up in numbers for the CityCenter project, which is not taking reservations yet.

So we find that people with money do not always throw it around. They run to places where their investments are safe. They are more sophisticated buyers than we have previously seen in the Las Vegas Valley and they have loudly voted. The condo craze has become a bust.

There is an important lesson in this for people who think that they can just show up in Las Vegas with money and take over the town. The scale of the poker game that is Las Vegas development is so great that no amount of outside money buys more than a seat at the table. And a seat alone is no promise of success. Investing on the Strip and its surroundings has taken a new direction.

July 23, 2006
Las Vegas Sun

20

An Ancient Incan Capital

Reflected in Las Vegas

ONE OF OUR PARTICULAR CONCEITS is that Las Vegas is unique among cities in human history. No parallels exist for our miracle in the desert, we like to gloat, and with good reason. It is improbable that any city grew so fast and achieved so much without producing more than smiles on people's faces.

You will never eat an apple from an orchard in the Las Vegas Valley—even though there is one—and you will never wear a sweater made from the wool of a sheep that grazed our fine grasses. We simply were not a viable part of that world.

I have been on a quest for parallels to Las Vegas. I simply can't believe that we are unique, that until Bugsy Siegel came along, no one ever thought of a city that made a ritual out of leisure. If there is nothing new under the sun, and usually there isn't, there has to be a precedent for Las Vegas.

I went to my friend, Andrew J. E. Bell, who teaches ancient history at UNLV. Bell told me that Las Vegas replicated the function of cities in the ancient world. In those days, people worked all year raising crops, and when the harvest was complete, they took their produce to the city to sell. Once there, they spent some time, perhaps taking a trip to the baths that dotted the ancient world or engaging the services of a prostitute or three. After such an indulgence, they went home, full of memories to hold them another year.

Pretty good parallel, but not perfect. That was the old Las Vegas, the stigmatized city of American folklore, the place your preacher warned you about. The new Las Vegas is more than simply a place to exchange money for service. It has also become famously ritualistic, part and parcel of the iconography of its society. People come to Las Vegas to be seen as well as to see it. They invest in it a marker of their accomplishment, as a way to announce they have arrived in the new century and are part of the future.

I continued my search and stumbled across Tiwanaku, an Incan capital high in the mountains of the Andes. Between 800 and 300 BC, the city flourished. Archaeologists once thought that Tiwanaku was an administrative center much like European imperial capitals, but recent work suggests a very different place.

Tiwanaku appears to have been a "cross between the Vatican and Disneyland," according to Charles Mann, author of *1491: New Revelations of the Americas before Columbus*. It had ceremonial connotations at the same time it had an extremely small population. Basically, Tiwanaku was populated by service workers, people who earned their keep by catering to visitors. Sound familiar?

Tiwanaku had another problem we know well. It, too, had to keep them coming back. Then as now, the premium was on the new, the fresh, the innovative. Tiwanaku was caught in the same predicament that we have, finding a way to anticipate desire rather than simply reflect it.

It also shared another Las Vegas trait: Tiwanaku tore down and rebuilt its core area time and again to achieve the illusion of the new. It had to, for its visitors, like ours, came to see the spectacle, to embrace the essence of their culture, and to experience something they could not get elsewhere.

Not surprisingly, Tiwanaku drew pilgrims by the thousands. Its visitors found what they wanted there, and most likely made the place into a canvas for their Andean neuroses. More than anything, this is Las Vegas's role for American and increasingly world society.

A few years ago, there was a documentary called *Holi-days*, about the way in which people made pilgrimages to Florence, Italy; Jerusalem, and Las Vegas. These are very different kinds of pilgrims, but the film made the case that the difference was only in the object of desire.

This argument heightens the parallels between Las Vegas and Tiwanaku. Our visitors seek redemption and reinvention, but usually not in a religious sense. Tiwanaku had strong religious connotations, for leisure was unknown in that world. But both drew pilgrims, in large numbers, and both kept them coming back by changing what they were. I wonder if Tiwanaku's service workers felt like ours. I wonder what caused the end of their world.

July 30, 2006
Las Vegas Sun

21

The Emerging Modern Cityscape

I MET AN AUSTRIAN FILM CREW at The District, easily greater Las Vegas's most successful mixed-use development to date. With its acres of parking, wonderful restaurants, concerts in the evening, and with the new Whole Foods complex across the street, it shines bright among the many developments we have seen in recent years. It could almost be a real town center. As they strolled the faux street, the men seemed impressed. One of them quipped: "It is very beautiful. It looks exactly like the village in the Alps where I grew up."

The District is one of two developments that encourage the suspension of disbelief in the best Las Vegas style. Like Lake Las Vegas, it creates the illusion of being better than real, subtly promising the fulfillment of desire. One canny local bicyclist jokes that his Sunday morning ride through the make-believe village by the lake is as close as he will ever get to the Tour de France. It may not be Europe, but in the right light, it feels awfully good.

But there is something unusual about both places. They are strangely unreal, as if they have countless visitors, but no residents. The signs of daily life are absent. The stores do not comprise a village. Instead they are all specialty endeavors, reminiscent of a mall, but in the open air. There is no hardware store, no place to get lumber or wallpaper, none of the things you would expect on any self-respecting Main Street.

This is the real difficulty as we make the transition from single-family homes to more dense forms of living in the Las Vegas Valley. Simply put, Americans are not used to living atop one another. We no longer have the kind of physical intimacy that we see in old movies such as Alfred Hitchcock's *Rear Window*, the classic where Jimmy Stewart spies on his neighbors from his wheelchair. The movie expresses a common way of life for urban Americans a half century ago. My students, largely born in the 1980s, could not believe that anyone ever lived like that.

The cityscape we have built so far will surely become denser, but the question of who will live in these new communities is entirely unsettled. To date, the great run-up in real estate prices has brought a new constituency to the valley, a more affluent group than we had previously seen. While this has been good for us so far, the boundaries of this group are increasingly apparent.

We don't know who will be buying the units in the proposed mixed-use developments. The main attraction here has been the opportunity to own a single-family home for a great deal less than the cost of one in coastal California. It remains to be seen whether future buyers crave a townhouse or a condo as much as a home, no matter how small the backyard.

We do know that most of the units in the existing mixed-use properties are strictly investments, purchased as play toys rather than homes. This poses all kinds of problems, not the least of which is the fact that no one really lives there.

We run the risk of building a new but vacant city, one without full-time residents. Think about it. What would any village, faux or real, be without its people? They are the essence of place, the key feature in giving any place its charm. Las Vegas works because we understand this critical precept.

The absence of permanent residents would put us in the remarkable position of hiring the next stage of the service economy, people who would pretend to live in the faux communities we will build. They would show up to work every day and "live" in these communities, shopping in the stores and populating the cafes for pay. They could play roles. Some might be students, others artists, still more ordinary working people. A script could govern the day, as it might at a living history museum such as Williamsburg, Virginia. How else would we continue the illusion of being better than real?

The goal of mixed-use developments is to create live, work, and play environments. We have got the play part down. The work part is coming along. The live piece is still a long way off.

August 20, 2006
Las Vegas Sun

22

One Step Ahead of the Game

BILL MURRAY USED TO GET a lot of laughs out of his caricature of the Las Vegas lounge singer, the smarmy crooner without even a droplet of sincerity in his soul. Like much about the image of our city, this hackneyed characterization has not stood the test of time. A bona fide lounge lizard himself, Murray has seen the changes firsthand. Las Vegas is home to the hippest club scene in the nation.

Las Vegas has been hip before. A moment of illusory sophistication accompanied the city's modern birth. Las Vegas entertainment began as center stage, with Jimmy Durante opening the Flamingo in 1946, Frank Sinatra's arrival at the Sands in 1952, and the interracial Moulin Rouge's brief moment at the pinnacle of afterhours cool in 1955. It peaked in the early 1960s with the Rat Pack and Louis Prima.

Then Las Vegas stumbled; instead of cutting edge it became middlebrow before the concept really existed. Las Vegas became Wayne Newton's town, where entertainment placated and did not challenge, a place so unhip that it was bound to become a caricature of whatever it intended. This was the era of Sonny and Cher, the town that originated the lounge singer, an icon that Murray parodied beyond cliché. After they got booted from television, Tony Orlando and Dawn headlined 1970s Las Vegas in their slide toward oblivion.

Even the opening of the Mirage and the inauguration of the Mirage Phase did not change entertainment at the club level. Focused on the big productions, Siegfried & Roy, Cirque de Soleil, and others, entertainment in Las Vegas moved toward the wide center of a growing market. Smaller hip venues did not fly.

The rebirth came out of nowhere. By 1995 a few small clubs began to alter the existing ethos, sneaking in under the radar of the enormous new hotels. The Metz Club, The Beach, and Drink and Eat Too attempted to draw a crowd of young conventioneers and tourists as well as locals.

The opening of the Hard Rock Hotel in March 1995 signaled a new Las Vegas, aimed at the young. A shrine for the rock 'n' roll generation, the Hard Rock began attempts to reach hip baby boomers. With its Stevie Ray Vaughn guitars and Sheryl Crow clothing on display, the Hard Rock opened the way to a different audience.

The smaller clubs had the market to themselves for a brief moment. Then the big hotels got wise to the fact that their patrons were escaping to other places because the entertainment on the premises was not quite to their liking. This was the age of *Swingers* and *Go*, movies that featured young rapscallions painting their dreams on the canvas of the new Las Vegas. The die was cast.

It happened quickly. In 1995 Club Rio atop the Rio opened the first hip nightclub inside a hotel. Other hotels looked at the niche and realized they had missed a significant opportunity. Not only could such clubs be lucrative, but they also promised cachet, a sense of hipness that would extend beyond the club to the rest of the property.

The year 1997 was the turning point. Two of the largest properties figured out an answer to the question of the 21–34 demographic. Upscale nightclubs Ra at the Luxor and Studio 54 at the MGM Grand were announced. Ra opened on New Year's Eve 1997. The two clubs showed that the model could work inside a hotel.

The MGM Grand and Luxor were not without precedent when they chose to create nightclubs. They did what corporate managers do best. They expropriated the ideas of smaller entrepreneurs and used their resources to create a better imitation of the original. They succeeded so completely that they changed the market.

From there, it was off to the races. Every major hotel soon had a hip nightclub and each was full of gyrating patrons. With the opening of the Palms, the city had a property devoted to the chic, where celebrities were visual currency. The ante went up and more clubs opened. No self-respecting Strip hotel would be caught dead without one. Once again, Las Vegas had done what the city does best: it anticipates desire where competitors only reflect it.

October 15, 2006
Las Vegas Sun

23

Las Vegas, the Chameleon City

THE CLOSING OF THE STARDUST RESORT and Casino on Wednesday and its transformation into Echelon Place, an upscale megaproperty replete with a hotel, condominiums, and other amenities, is the latest chapter in the never-ending reinvention of Las Vegas. Like no other city in the United States—indeed the world—Las Vegas creates itself anew in the wink of an eye. That malleability is one major component of the alchemy of the place, but by no means the only reason for the remarkable rebirth of what was once the nation's "Sin City."

In two decades, Las Vegas has gone from gaming to tourism to entertainment. In the same span, the metropolitan area nearly quadrupled in population, as Las Vegas took a primary place in the top tier of U.S. cities. Most amazing, this evolution occurred as gaming spread throughout the nation after passage of the Indian Gaming Regulatory Act in 1988. The city that everybody has long loved to deride must be doing something right.

The transition has been rapid. Two generations ago, modern Las Vegas was born with the sophisticated cachet of Sin City for the nightclub set, which quickly degenerated into kitsch. Only a generation ago, in the late 1970s and early 1980s, the city retained its stigma as the sleazy home of tawdry sex and mobsters. Las Vegas seemed played out, passé, soon to be cast aside as a flimsy relic of a laced-up morality.

One of the last of the first generation of Las Vegas hotels, the Stardust had its own checkered history. It was the scene of the convoluted events of the book and movie *Casino*, the story of the last great mob scandal in Las Vegas. The Boyd Gaming Corporation acquired the property after the body of Tony Spilotro, the onetime mob boss of Las Vegas, turned up in Indiana, paving the way for the property's transformation.

Las Vegas the city has made a living out of reinventing itself. Its consistent reinvention, once scorned as flimsy and fraudulent, shaped its trajectory from periphery to mainstream and has become a much-envied trait.

Las Vegas's physical limitations forced the community to bend to the will of whatever enterprise would generate revenues. This submission to the inevitability of change gave Las Vegas a fluidity, a way around the rules of midcentury America, that locals have learned to treasure. The city learned that its shape was always transitory, always flexible, not only because it responded to the emotions of mainstream culture, but also because the forces behind the city were on the borders of legality. Even in moments of great success, Las Vegas had a powerful sense of impermanence, a strong intuition that whatever ruled today might well not tomorrow.

From its roots in sin, Las Vegas has grown into the most malleable tourist destination on the planet. It makes the visitor, however ordinary, the center of the story, holding up a figurative mirror and asking: "What do you want to be, and what will you pay to be it?" Who you were or what you were yesterday makes little difference. All tourist towns reflect desire—but Las Vegas anticipates it.

To the surprise of many, entertainment, not gaming, is redefining Las Vegas this time. Gambling dollars grease the wheels, but since 1996, gambling has accounted for less than half the money spent by visitors to Vegas, according to state economic data. The city offers the middle-class visitor a luxury experience at a middle-class price. It also can cater to the most uncompromising of expense accounts. As the *New York Times* recently reported, this town that was once synonymous with cheap buffets led the charge (along with New York) into the era of the $40 entrée.

With more than 40 million visitors annually, the shoulder season is short.

Entertainment has created a city like many others and simultaneously apart. Las Vegas is equal parts Washington, D.C. (a transient place where everyone is on the make), Los Angeles or Miami (more and more conversations are in Spanish), Phoenix (almost 25 percent of the population is retired, and medical care has become a huge industry), Detroit of the old days (home of a vocal and powerful semiskilled unionized work force), and New Orleans before Katrina (as Etta James still sings, "Care forgot, where everybody parties a lot."). And Las Vegas is newer, less structured, more vital, with fewer rules and wider degrees of what constitutes normal.

Along the way and almost by accident, Las Vegas has become the place where the twenty-first century begins, the first spectacle of the postmodern world. In this incarnation, the old pariah becomes the model, the colony of everywhere, the colonizer of its former masters. Old Nevada allowed people to come and cast off their sins. When professional prizefighting was illegal in every state in the union but one, Nevada filled the void with title bouts.

This once dubious trait—liberation from the burden of sin—is a virtue in the postindustrial world. Las Vegas was the first city devoted to the consumption of entertainment, and to be first at anything in a fluid culture is to have a claim on being significant. It offers an economic model for cities, states, and regions looking to create their own economic panacea—even as they hold their noses.

Las Vegas as spectacle has become the rhythm of America, combining holidays, rituals, and ceremonials: Martin Luther King Jr. Day, the Super Bowl, Chinese New Year, Presidents Day weekend, March Madness and especially the Final Four, Memorial Day, the NBA finals, Fourth of July, Labor Day, the NFL season, the World Series, Halloween, Thanksgiving, Christmas, and New Year's Eve. Anybody's holiday or event will do. Every night can be New Year's Eve if you want it to be.

Doomsayers all predict the demise of Las Vegas, arguing that the appetite it satisfies will diminish or that so many other places will offer

Las Vegas–style amenities that the city will lose its singular luster. But if Las Vegas's history is any guide, the city's ability to respond to cultural change will keep it vigorous. Since the legalization of gambling in Nevada in 1931, Las Vegas has provided Americans with what they weren't supposed to have at home and make whatever it was permissible if not flat-out OK. This sleight of hand was a neat trick, accomplished by the city's fundamental pliability.

In Las Vegas, ordinary people feel special, and people who feel they are special can be catered to in a manner that suits their self-indulgence. Las Vegas anticipated the transformation of American culture not out of innate savvy but as a result of a lack of other options for the city. The reinvention of American culture as purely the self—it's all about you—catapulted Las Vegas to prominence. The city took sin and made it a choice, a sometimes ambiguous choice that many in U.S. society, from the privileged to the ordinary, couldn't handle, but choice nonetheless. Combined with a visionary approach to experience that melded Hollywood and Americans' taste for comfort and self-deception, Las Vegas grew into the last American frontier city, as foreign at times as Prague but as quintessential as Peoria.

In Las Vegas, you can choose your fantasy. In the rest of America, you don't always get to pick.

October 29, 2006
Los Angeles Times

As Real As It Gets. Photo by Virgil Hancock III.

Part II

Las Vegas
as Community

Introduction

Nevada Must End Public Poverty

IT IS TIME FOR NEVADA to grow up at last. Look around. We're a big-time state now, an important player in the West and in the nation, but we're still stuck with the governmental mechanisms of an earlier time. The worst by far is our tax system, regressive to its core. Not only does it fail to generate the revenue a growing state needs, it also disproportion- ately penalizes the less well-off. We've long avoided our responsibility to ourselves—at great peril to the state—simply because we could.

Nevada began as an individualists' paradise and it is still the place where your property is your property more than anywhere else in the Union. Our unique historic circumstances, the small and spread-out population, the preponderance of federal land, and the early recogni- tion that Nevada could sustain itself by providing services frowned upon elsewhere, lulled us into a comatose state. It allowed us to partici- pate in the fiction that made freedom into a lack of social obligation. With only one hundred and fifty thousand people in 1950, who cared? Nevadans were a hardy and self-reliant bunch. We didn't ask for any- thing we couldn't get on our own.

Then we started to grow. Over the last two decades, everything about the state, especially its demography, changed—but our archaic tax system didn't.

Taxes were anathema in the individualists' paradise, where the government that governed best governed not at all. A small state with few people didn't need much to run itself and it shied away from asking for more, afraid that people and business would leave if compelled to pay their share. State leaders dreaded a reprise of the late nineteenth century, when population dropped so far that even retaining statehood seemed dubious. The twentieth-century dollars from federal projects such as Hoover Dam and the Nevada Test Site made it easy to sustain the illusion that we didn't have to pay. The result: Nevadans proudly did for themselves, ignoring the incongruity that sustained them and creating a haven that drew others of similar disposition.

When taxes became necessary, it was easy to concoct a system that let visitors pay a large share. With a constitutional amendment against a state income tax, the choices were limited. The 6.25 percent gaming tax was one linchpin, and, until the early 1980s, the property tax made up another. It was a small stool of state revenue, but a fairly stable one.

Then Governor Bob List committed the original sin of Nevada taxation. Feeling the cold wind blowing east after Proposition 13 in California and trying to save a few bucks for his land-rich cronies in the north, List shifted Nevada away from property tax to sales tax.

The result has been perennial instability in revenue. Sales tax revenue depends on consumer spending; the seven hundred thousand or so people in Nevada in 1980 certainly didn't spend enough to pay the state's bills. But, the reasoning went, visitors who have come in ever-increasing numbers since might not even notice they were filling state coffers. Throughout the 1980s and 1990s, we became accustomed to this fiction, ignoring its impact on the state. The visitors kept buying and all seemed well.

All tourist markets ultimately become real estate markets and a lot of those visitors returned to stay, especially in Las Vegas. The savvy among them recognized that in Nevada, it was easy to lay off the cost of your existence—all the things a modern state required, especially education and social services—on someone else. People who felt this was a good thing self-selected to move to Nevada, providing a powerful constituency that opposed anything that cost money. In the process, they slaughtered the goose that laid their particular golden egg: they came in such numbers that they overwhelmed the old system.

We've reached a critical juncture: our traditions and our future have collided full force. As the state's demography has changed, we've simultaneously become older and younger. More children and more retirees mean more people who need services and who contribute less to state coffers. The diminishing group in the middle, the ones who make up the work force, bear a larger proportion of the burden every day. As we resemble the dreaded peak-valley-peak population structure, the very one that is impoverishing Japan and has begun to do damage to western Europe, the need for a change becomes more acute. Now we have to make a difficult choice: do we continue with the status quo, failing as it is, or do we invent a new solution that leads to a brighter future?

No individual in Nevada pays his or her way, not me, not you. The combination of sales tax and property tax simply does not cover the cost of what we receive. Everybody who moves here takes more out of the system than they put back in. Growth doesn't pay for itself either. The dollars from it this year might well cover 1982's expenditures. As my friend, the distinguished historian Gene Moehring says, "It is public poverty and private prosperity here."

Nevada needs a revised tax structure. In a state that is diversifying, gaming shouldn't be expected to pay for everything else. It is time we grew up and shouldered our own freight. Doing so will slow the decline in quality of life we're experiencing, if for no other reason than it will make the next group of freeloaders coming down the road a little less likely to want to stay.

January 23, 2003
Las Vegas Mercury

24

The Rebirth of Bugsy Siegel?

FOR THE BETTER PART of the last decade, we've all engaged in a weird little sport, trying to gauge exactly when the boom, what I call the "Mirage Phase," will end and what will follow. Every new hotel that opened prompted claims that this was it, this was the one that would saturate the market, would drive the room occupancy rate down, push resort/casino stock prices way down, and cut into the cash machine that entertainment-based Las Vegas had become. Time and again we were all wrong; the Monte Carlo, New York, New York, Mandalay Bay, Paris, Bellagio, the Venetian, and on and on all opened and instead of bust, we got more of everything, more visitors, more hotels, more restaurants, more shopping, more shows. Some called each of the hotels the straw that would break the camel's back. Each time the camel stood, back unswayed. Most of us gave up trying to predict the end and with good reason. We'd all been wrong so many times that it seemed silly, and as John L. Smith says, "If you predict the end of the world every day, sooner or later you're going to be right!"

The Mirage Phase did come to an end, but in a way no one expected. Steve Wynn, whose empire seemed impenetrable, sold his properties to the MGM this past spring and Las Vegas became a completely corporate town. The vulnerability of his stock prices forced his hand. Publicly traded companies respond to the impact of their decisions on their quarterly earnings before interest, taxes, depreciation, and amortization (EBITDA) and they completely dominated the city. Wynn got caught with his stock at a low point and could do little to block the MGM's takeover. With that purchase instead of innovative entrepreneurs who fashioned the conceptual future and then watched as corporate money scarfed up their ideas, Las Vegas became a city full of publicly traded companies that cared mostly about the bottom line.

In the process, a series of new doors opened up. The level of return that the biggest players—MGM/Mirage, Mandalay Bay, and Park Place—demand and the size of their empires has raised the bar for participation at their level and conversely created new niches rather than closing them up. It's as if the corporate radar screen has risen higher and diminished the value of properties that are inherently lucrative to the biggest groups. A combination of seemingly easy profit and a need for status have brought all kinds of people into that area beneath the radar, where an entire range of well-heeled entrepreneurs have once again descended on Las Vegas and are trying to make it their own.

This phenomenon has happened so many times here that it wouldn't deserve comment, except that the targets these new entrepreneurs are seeking are precisely the midtier properties of the biggest chains. Steve Wynn's purchase of the Desert Inn is the prototype. Ed Roski's purchase of the Las Vegas Hilton is more typical of what seems likely to follow. Both assets were diminished in the eyes of their previous owners, but both clearly promised profit and were significant enough for their new owners to see a way to make an impact on the market. In essence, Wynn's purchase of the Desert Inn allowed him to function without worrying about the EBITDA, to run a hotel as he felt it should, not as the stock analysts on Wall Street and his shareholders wanted him to. In short, Wynn, Roski, and other such entrepreneurs, not subject to all the constraints of publicly traded companies, could run these properties for service, not for the raw numbers of the bottom line.

This could kick off a new era of innovation that has the ability to redefine the city even better than it is. The rise of entrepreneurial owners mirrors the traits of the moments of Las Vegas's greatest success, when visionary individuals created the context into which corporate money poured and growth followed. That's why it's called the "Mirage

Phase," not the Hilton phase or something similar. The corporations that owned hotels by the 1980s were well endowed with cash, but lacked imagination. They weren't entertainers, they were hotels and they followed . . . each other around in a circle. The two towers built at the Flamingo in 1972 and 1977 typified the breed. Architecture critic Alan Hess says architects Rissman and Rissman's 1972 addition "could have been taken for an office building anywhere in the country," and with the second tower, Bugsy Siegel's pool, the pinnacle of his bizarre idea of class, was in the shade all day long.

The rebirth of the individual entrepreneur less subjected to the pull of the capital markets offers a blueprint for consolidation to follow the massive outburst of building. It creates a revival of the kind of ethos that began with Bugsy Siegel and continued through Jay Sarno and Steve Wynn. Instead of building anew, this stage may see the reinvention of the midtier properties with the verve of the Mirage Phase.

There's a flip side of course. Siegel was a megalomaniac who made money in other—illegal—endeavors and used the Flamingo as a sop to his ego, a way of proclaiming his importance to the Hollywood that rejected him. There's a quality of intoxicating hubris in this model, a certain amount of substituting money for sense. If this wave of newcomers does the same as its predecessors, they could misread the market like Bob Snow did at the old Main Street and end up erecting expensive monuments to the self.

Either way, it's a new era. The Mirage Phase, the era of the megaresorts, is ending, at least for now. Its dinosaur baby, the new Aladdin, struggled to open and may find that last born is a dangerous position. Like any industry, casino-hotels are fundamentally imitative; they look around and have to have what their peers have. The introduction of entrepreneurs with smaller amounts of capital than the biggest groups may be a good thing. It may spur corporate Las Vegas to better innovation, to the use of its vast capital in more responsive ways, to push the envelope further and keep us the leading destination on the planet.

I once likened Steve Wynn to a guy on a bicycle leading great semi-trucks of capital to new heights of creativity. That version of our recent history has given this city its best economic moments. Its reprise may not be a bad thing at all.

October 2000
Las Vegas CityLife

25

Del Webb's Impact

THE OPENING OF THE Del E. Webb Middle School last week is a belated but fitting tribute to a man whose career illustrates the entrepreneurial energy that Las Vegas rewards. In a town where schools are named after the living, the recognition accorded Webb is long overdue. Webb's personal career was a classic American story, and the company he founded remains a major player in Las Vegas and the Southwest more than thirty years after his death. In many ways, the story of the building of modern Las Vegas starts with Del E. Webb and the corporation he founded; in equally many, Webb was instrumental in paving the path to today.

Born the scion of a wealthy Fresno, California, family in 1899, the young Del Webb aspired to be a baseball player. At six feet tall and almost two hundred pounds, he was a substantive man by the standards of his time. He had some success as a pitcher, but was driven from the game by a bout with typhoid fever that he contracted during an exhibition game at San Quentin Prison in California. He entered construction after recovering from the illness.

After a successful career in the 1930s and 1940s building federal projects as diverse as courthouses and Japanese internment camps, Webb came to Las Vegas after World War II. The Valley National Bank of Phoenix, which held a $600,000 note from Billy Wilkerson, the impresario who started the Flamingo, called him to help them out of a difficult situation. Both Webb and a Las Vegas mobster, Gus Greenbaum, were close to the bank, and as Wilkerson floundered, Webb stepped in to protect the bank's investment. The powerful construction magnate found himself in a different sphere, one where

Ben "Bugsy" Siegel called the shots.

It was a funny match. Siegel was extravagant and bizarre, given to fits of anger and hasty and permanent solutions to even the smallest of problems; Webb was an opportunistic and efficient builder with an eye on the bottom line. Their relationship was always stormy, and the threat of violence permeated the air. Almost every account of their interaction contains a version of Siegel's reassurance that mobsters "only kill each other" in response to Webb's visible alarm at the twelve notches on the gangster's figurative gunbelt. Webb was apparently not too intimidated. Las Vegas legend attributes much of the cost overrun at the Flamingo Hotel to Webb's men checking materials in at the front gate, billing them to Siegel, and then driving them out the back gate to other Webb jobs.

From the Flamingo, Webb moved on to build countless Las Vegas hotels, high schools, civic buildings, and other structures throughout the 1950s, paving the way for even greater involvement in Las Vegas and its primary industry at the time, casino gambling. In a 1961 transaction, the Del Webb Company gained control of the Sahara. The construction magnate was now a casino owner, and by 1965, the company had more than $60 million invested in Nevada.

With this transaction, Del Webb foreshadowed the future of Las Vegas in important ways. He was a legitimate businessman who recognized the potential of gambling as a lucrative industry and blended prominent national business endeavors with an intimate relationship to Nevada and its quirky rules and laws. Webb and Dan Topping had purchased the New York Yankees in 1945, owning them during the great years of the 1950s and through the 1964 season. Sports betting was technically legal in 1960s Las Vegas, but a 10 percent federal tax on sports wagers kept most action off the books. The specter of gambling hung over professional sports like a cloud. In 1963, NFL stars Paul Hornung and Alex Karras were suspended for an entire season for betting and baseball stars like Mickey Mantle and Whitey Ford were notorious for their drinking, carousing, and gambling.

Webb circumvented ostensible concerns about casino ownership by devising a system of operating companies that leased the casinos from the corporation. This solved the problem of bringing stockholders in front of the gaming board. It also provided cover for his ownership of the Yankees. As far as straightlaced Major League Baseball was concerned, Del Webb owned the ball club but not the casino; the Nevada Gaming Commission willingly affirmed this fiction. The Sahara became a profitable venture for the company, and Webb bought other casinos, including the Thunderbird, the Mint in downtown Las Vegas, and a new casino at Lake Tahoe.

Webb also maintained a close relationship with Howard Hughes. The two men had been friends long before Hughes retreated into his drug-addicted solitude, and even after, the recluse would meet with Webb on occasion. Webb handled much business from Hughes, by some accounts more than $1 billion worth. As Hughes's empire divested itself of casinos, Webb and his successors scooped up a number of properties. Although Webb himself died in 1974, his company became the major player in Nevada gaming. By 1978, Del Webb Company employed seven thousand gaming workers and was the largest employer in the state.

Del Webb's recent impact in Las Vegas came from another dimension of the company's business, housing. When suburbanization swept the nation after World War II, led by Levittown on Long Island, outside of New York City, construction companies around the country built new homes by the thousands. Until the Sahara deal, Webb had focused on commercial construction in Las Vegas and the residential retirement community of Sun City outside Phoenix. By the time the company began to divest itself of its casinos, the housing market in Las Vegas had new energy. In the 1980s, a changing market upset the conventions of Las Vegas Valley and the Webb Company became the catalyst in a regional transformation. The combination of the Sun City model and the Webb Company's willingness to act as if gaming was no different than any other industry inaugurated the wholesale suburbanization of Las Vegas.

The Del Webb Company's subsequent role in Las Vegas is well-known. From Summerlin to Sun City Anthem, the company has been one of the prime builders of the great burst that has defined the past twenty years. Its role especially in the retirement market has been prescient, for company leaders recognized the value of the retirement economy well ahead of much of the rest of the industry and even of the nation.

But what set Del Webb apart was his ability to translate the level of economic opportunity in a despised industry into a profitable and respectable enterprise. In the 1960s, no one doubted that there was money to be made in gaming, but the New York Stock Exchange would not touch the industry no matter how it was packaged. Owning the New York Yankees at a time when gambling was a vice instead of a recreational choice and adding a prominent Las Vegas casino to his holdings without incurring the ire of either Major League Baseball or the national press was bold and unprecedented. It foreshadowed the brilliant future we have since experienced. Webb paved the way for the Maloofs' simultaneous ownership of the Palms and the NBA's Sacramento Kings and in the end for the eventual presence of a major league franchise of some type in Las Vegas. Always unconventional, he thought ahead of the game and took actions that seeded the path to Las Vegas's respectability. Las Vegas has always rewarded innovation and creativity. In Webb's case, the public tribute took a great deal longer than the economic reward.

September 23, 2005
Las Vegas Business Press

26

Stay off TASC

COLORADO'S RECENT SUSPENSION of its Taxpayers' Bill of Rights (TABOR) is the first sign of common sense in a public vote in a long time. Like Proposition 13 in California, passed in 1978, TABOR is a slick manipulation of a gullible, fearful, self-interested, and uninformed public. Simultaneously, it is an unmitigated public policy disaster.

With the stunningly appealing name of Taxpayers' Bill of Rights, TABOR purported to be a hedge against wasteful government spending and the creation of new government programs. Modeled on California's Proposition 13, TABOR allowed state government to spend more than it had in the previous year, but only to the level of inflation and the increase in population.

While an appealing model, this formula held in it a ticking time bomb. TABOR worked reasonably well during flush times. Between 1997 and 2002, more than $3.2 billion was returned to Colorado taxpayers.

But even during good economic times, the state was unable to remain competitive in the funding of its education system. Even more, upkeep of roads, state health care and Medicare funding, and other necessities lagged.

TABOR did not allow Colorado to make the improvements in its infrastructure and in its education system to continue to recruit new talent to the state economy, a precursor of a continuously improving economy. It was penny wise and pound foolish.

When economic growth slowed, the problems with TABOR became apparent. TABOR did not allow Colorado to create a Rainy Day fund of the kind so important in balancing the state budget.

The shortcomings in education led to passage in 1997 of Amendment 23, a funding measure for education that outstripped the spending limits that TABOR established. The result was a tax-reduction measure that had the parallel impact of creating a permanent shortfall at the same time it eroded the very entities that could promote economic growth.

There is much talk about a similar measure in Nevada called the Tax and Spending Control initiative, which goes by the acronym TASC. The recent housing boom and the increase in real estate taxes, deftly handled by the Nevada Legislature in 2005, have created the same kind of pressure that Californians experienced in the 1970s. Proposition 13, which capped real estate taxes after a similar spike in housing values, serves as an instructive lesson for us.

No single piece of legislation did more damage to California and its status as the leading American state than Proposition 13. Even though it is the fifth largest economy in the world, the Golden State is continuously seeking new sources of funding for its schools, roads, and universities.

Its social service burden, so much greater than Nevada's that it defies comprehension, grows as governors as diverse as Pete Wilson and Arnold Schwarzenegger struggled to find ways to meet obligations.

Nevada remains in the bottom quarter of state tax burdens in the United States. By the Tax Foundation's reckoning, in 2005 we are thirty-eighth in tax burden with a rating of 9.5—with 1 being the highest. In 1974 Nevada was the tenth most highly taxed state in the nation at 10.5 percent of income. We are almost exactly where we were in 1989, when the great boom began. That year, Nevada ranked thirty-seventh with the same 9.5 tax-burden rating that we have today.

In contrast, Nevada remains in the bottom three in almost every social service category. Our extremely limited state safety net already has great big holes. Nevada is a bad place to be if you are poor, mentally ill, sick without insurance, or need other state assistance. We serve best the citizens who can already take care of themselves.

Now I have long argued that you need a microscope to find your tax burden in Nevada. Plenty of people will disagree with me, especially those on fixed incomes. But the truth remains: if you want services—even police, fire, and especially medicine—you have to pay taxes.

Our tax system is still dysfunctional. Sales tax and casino tax make up 75 percent of state revenue. That has created a typical Nevada dependency on outsiders to pay a large part of our share of running the state.

The system is also regressive; poor people pay the same taxes as the more well-off, effectively pushing the burden down the socioeconomic ladder. While Nevada thankfully does not tax food, sales tax is the most regressive form of taxation.

In the end, the people who push for something like TABOR or Proposition 13 either do not understand Nevada's situation or think they can get elected by spreading fear. We're already cut to the bone.

The question is not how to cap taxes, but how to use the tax dollars we have to further the diversification of the state economy. That's the question I'd like to see gubernatorial candidates and those running for Congress answer.

November 13, 2005
Las Vegas Sun

27

Splitting the School District

ONCE AGAIN, THE PROSPECT of dividing the Clark County School District into a series of Balkanized provinces has reared its ugly head.

This maneuver would not only resegregate the Clark County School District, but it would also create a real division between haves and have-nots at precisely a moment when other economic conditions, such as the price of housing, are pushing the community apart.

I cannot imagine why anyone would think this is a good idea.

Not surprisingly, the source of this is state Senator Sandra Tiffany, who for more than a decade has brought this topic up time and again.

Tiffany's motivations are obvious: she represents a part of the Las Vegas Valley with comparatively high household income that could be the basis of a well-funded suburban school district that would gain at the expense of the rest of the valley in any division of the district.

Her Henderson-based district would have all kinds of advantages. If Tiffany could tie districts to their tax base, hers and other suburban districts would be able to fund students at a much higher level than the state currently provides.

With a more affluent base from which to draw, they would also be able to benefit from the generosity of parents and nearby businesses, creating the kind of powerful suburban school districts that exist around most major American cities.

I live in Tiffany's district, but I couldn't be more opposed to the division of the school district. Despite its obvious flaws, the school district does a remarkable job of projecting and then managing the phenomenal growth that we see every day. In each of the past fifteen years, we have added enough students to equal roughly the average American school district.

While our overall test scores are not impressive, what we've been able to do is. We have built more schools than we can count and assimilated thousands of new students, many of whom bring real academic and social problems with them. We've been able to create the beginning of a system that provides educational opportunity widely across the community.

Students who bring pathologies from other places do not necessarily succeed here, and this should not surprise anyone. What is important is that the context in which they can succeed exists. Only a large, well-funded school district can provide that.

Breaking up the school district would become an administrative nightmare.

A series of smaller districts would be forced to compete with one another for resources. Each would have a separate administration, a remarkable drain of resources in a state where education is perennially underfunded.

Waves of administrators would replace teachers as each district tried to meet the tsunami of misguided federal legislation like No Child Left Untested—oops, I mean No Child Left Behind. Each district's educational opportunities would suffer.

In a world where teachers are scarce in the valley and we must recruit as many as two thousand each year from outside our borders, competition among the districts for teachers would be fierce.

Given the funding formula, ultimately the competition would extend to students as well. Districts would offer incentives to students to jump boundaries, always with an eye on the state funding formula.

Smaller districts would not be able to offer the wide variety of opportunities currently available in public schools. They would be more like private schools, trumpeting their successes while only being able to provide them within narrow realms. The bleating would be constant; the attempts to maximize each district's position against the others ongoing.

Magnet schools and projects like the Las Vegas Academy would be hard to sustain. The arts and sports would suffer, for smaller districts are notorious for their inability to sustain athletic programs. The great tradition of Las Vegas high school sports would surely diminish.

The trend in the valley is toward the dissolution of community-wide institutions and their reinvention as neighborhood-based entities. For truly local entities, churches, sports leagues, and the like, this makes sense.

Tearing apart the school district is a craven effort to extend privilege to the privileged. Our problem is not the size of the school district. It's the amount of funding the schools receive and the unfunded mandates that are yokes around our collective neck. We remain fifth lowest in the nation in per pupil school funding. Let's start by fixing that problem.

November 27, 2005
Las Vegas Sun

28

Why Elvis Grew into Las Vegas

TODAY IS ELVIS PRESLEY'S BIRTHDAY, and it should be an official holiday in Las Vegas. Every year we should stop for a moment and remember the King.

No entertainer symbolized the city better than Elvis. No one is more closely associated with us than the King.

He gave us "Viva Las Vegas," our signature song, and spawned generations of impersonators. They not only offer every manifestation of Elvis, from the sex symbol to the middle-aged man, but they also imbue the city with a good-natured kitsch that makes us lovable in a way that no other city, not even Elvis's hometown of Memphis, Tennessee, can be.

When Elvis first played Las Vegas in 1956, he was twenty-one years old and on the way up, still young, ripped, and taut, not the blimp-like caricature he later became. The booking came at the last minute, and Elvis found himself in the thousand-seat Venus Room at the New Frontier. Freddy Martin and his orchestra backed the band.

By March, 1956 had already been a good year for Elvis and the neon city of excess promised more, so much more. In pure Las Vegas style, a twenty-four-foot-high cutout of the rising star appeared in front of the New Frontier. Las Vegas could always recognize a star and roll out the red carpet.

But Elvis bombed. For two weeks, he, guitarist Scotty Moore, bass player Bill Black, and drummer D. J. Fontana were "a very nervous, very out-of-place hillbilly quartet," in the words of biographer Peter Guralnick.

Elvis even introduced one of his hits as "Heartburn Hotel." They just did not fit, too raw for the older, sophisticated Las Vegas audience. One guest bounced up from a ringside table, shouted that the music was too loud, and headed for the casino. Elvis was the fringe, and Las Vegas only did well with the center.

In 1956 the stamp of Las Vegas signaled Elvis's emergence from the ghetto of hillbilly and his arrival in the larger market. But it cost him something, too, both immediately and in the long term.

After two and a half years of girls screaming, he finally reached a little Waterloo, a place where his act didn't fly, where the audience turned him back. Scotty Moore thought "people that were there, if you'd lifted them out and taken them to San Antonio, the big coliseum, they'd have been going crazy," but he was wrong.

A Las Vegas audience in 1956 was not made up of teenagers, didn't hail from the Bible Belt, and was not starved for entertainment.

When Elvis returned in 1969, he was a real star. He began a record seven-year stay, performing 837 sold-out shows in a row at Kirk Kerkorian's International Hotel, which became the Las Vegas Hilton. After the rock 'n' roll revolution, Elvis finally fit Las Vegas. The years and the changes in society conspired to make him the first nostalgic act, perfect for the Las Vegas of 1969.

Elvis loved Las Vegas as much as the city came to love him. There was plenty to do, and a guy who didn't sleep much didn't have to worry about the town closing down on him. He also recognized a future in Las Vegas, a promise that an audience that rejected him in 1956 would love him a decade or more down the road. This failure with a future became the paradox and promise of the City of Entertainment.

Las Vegas entertainment still rings truer at the box office than in the coffeehouses. The city takes malleable art and fixes it, making it palatable to the widest possible audience. While this is great for business, it's hard on performers, even, and maybe especially, on Elvis.

Even today, Las Vegas doesn't nurture entertainment; it only buys it. Las Vegas validates performers but has yet to genuinely create entertainment. An artist can hold the town, can become it, but Las

Vegas pushes artists and compromises them at the same time.

Las Vegas packages experience to the widest audience it can reach. More people saw Elvis in the showroom of the Las Vegas Hilton than anywhere else in the world. But what they saw in the fading star was a memory, a package, a wrapper for desires that they once held or to which they still aspired.

So when we remember Elvis, we should also remember what it took for him to succeed here as well.

January 8, 2006
Las Vegas Sun

29

Betting on the Super Bowl

IT IS ALMOST AS HARD to remember a time when the Super Bowl was not a national event as it is to recall a time when Las Vegas was not chic.

The NFL would deny this, but the rise of the Super Bowl and that of Las Vegas are different sides of the same coin, evolutionary processes that are closely linked as gambling became gaming and the United States devoted itself to leisure and self-indulgence.

Gambling built both—not the NFL, you say, but it's true—and both have become postmodern entertainment. When Mick Jagger shakes his grandfatherly backside at halftime after a full week of all kinds of entertainment in midwinter Detroit, what was once a football game has become more than a sporting event.

It is a popular culture icon, a star that burns brightly in the American sky. This year's Super Bowl even touts an environmental program, to keep the event "cleaner and greener, and to lessen the impact on the local and global environment."

It wasn't always so. The first Super Bowl, in Los Angeles in January 1967, was not even a sellout. Only 61,496 people watched the Packers demolish the Chiefs in the 100,000-seat Los Angeles Coliseum. As late as 1972, you could walk up on game day and buy a ticket. The league has come a long way.

But not so far that it doesn't fear its roots. The NFL was always a gambler's league. The great names, Tim Mara, Art Rooney, Charles W. Bidwill, who owned the then-Chicago, later St. Louis, and eventually and pathetically, the Arizona Cardinals, Sonny Werblin of the Jets, Carroll Rosenblum of the Colts, and others all had ties to the world of gambling. Such figures are so far in the past that you would think no one cares . . . but the NFL does.

For my money, this explains why the NFL is so consistently and fundamentally hostile to Las Vegas. It won't broadcast our commercials, it went out of its way to mess with Super Bowl parties here—and nowhere else—and it even challenged the right of satellite owners to broadcast the game. This hatred is pathological.

The NFL sees in its past the only conceivable threat to its future. The league has been dogged by betting scandals since the 1940s: Frankie Filchock, Paul Hornung and Alex Karras, and Art Schlichter stand out, but they are only the tip of the iceberg. There have certainly been plenty more. Betting is the lifeblood of football. Gambling maintains the fever pitch of fan intensity. Do you really think that grown men would paint their distended bellies in their team's colors and stand in subzero weather without their shirts if they didn't have money riding on the game? There isn't enough alcohol in the world . . .

The flaw in the NFL's logic is that betting on its games everywhere but here feeds the coffers of all kinds of illegal enterprises. For all its money and power, the league always has one eye on the point spread. It has no idea what kind of influences its players are subjected to.

At least now, players make enough money that they're harder to buy than in the past, but wealthy young men still have their problems. It makes a lot more sense to embrace legalized sports betting operations like we have in Las Vegas than to tacitly condone an illegal infrastructure with tentacles throughout the nation.

But the NFL cannot stomach this because it refuses to recognize that Las Vegas and the league are twins, mirror images of one another. Both rose from tawdry obscurity to the limelight as culture loosened and as they successfully negotiated the changes in American society from deferred gratification to instant adulation of the self.

When players say NFL stands for "No Fun League," they are usually complaining about edicts against flamboyant celebration. But they've hit the NFL's problem on the nose: the league wants the money, power, and fame that comes with being the nation's premier sport, but it fears precisely the attributes that won it that exalted position.

Even though NFL Commissioner Paul Tagliabue would turn pale at the prospect, the league should look to Las Vegas to see how to handle that double-edged sword. Since Wall Street has funded Las Vegas hotels, they've become the only thing in America more expensive than an NFL franchise.

February 5, 2006
Las Vegas Sun

30

Invest Big in the Convention Center

IF YOU HAD LOOKED AROUND IN 1988, when the Indian Gaming Regulatory Act became law, you might have guessed that Las Vegas's future was dicey. Until then the Silver State enjoyed a near monopoly on legalized betting in the United States. Only New Jersey permitted anything more than a lottery.

But in 1988, Atlantic City posed a genuine threat to Las Vegas. Closer to seemingly infinite numbers of people—Atlantic City is an easy bus ride from New York, Boston, Philadelphia, Washington, D.C., and Baltimore—the once-queen of American leisure seemed likely to snatch the crown back from Las Vegas.

Indian gaming potentially posed an even greater threat. Instead of a few casinos on the other coast, Indian gaming promised an infinite number of places scattered across the country. The presumption at the time was that all these little grind joints would draw people away from Las Vegas.

Of course, that's not what happened. Indian gaming and even Atlantic City turned into feeders for Las Vegas. Beginning with the Mirage, we embarked on the most remarkable bit of urban construction ever undertaken. In the decade between the opening of the Mirage in 1989 and the completion of the Aladdin in 2000, Las Vegas built more than sixty thousand hotel rooms, as many as are in Los Angeles. The new Las Vegas was born, and we are much the better for it.

In the end, the piece of legislation that was supposed to bury Las Vegas, the Indian Gaming Regulatory Act, coincides with the greatest building boom in Las Vegas's history. Indian gaming really did turn out to be spring training for Las Vegas. No one ever came to Las Vegas and then said: "Now that I've seen Las Vegas, I've really got to go to Foxwoods!"

In the process, we made ourselves into something new, with 1989 serving as a breakpoint, a sea change between past and present. Before that time, Las Vegas was primarily about gaming. After the opening of the Mirage, we became the city of entertainment, the place where people went to see what was hot. Gaming ceased to be the menu; it remained a prominent entrée among many other choices.

This offered economic rewards few anticipated. Between 1989 and 2004, Las Vegas roughly doubled its annual visitation, from a little more than 18 million to more than 37 million. At the same time, the "visitor dollar contribution," a measure of what visitors spend here, roughly tripled. We got more visitors, sure; what's more important is that we got more out of them.

But this kind of success posed a larger problem: how to maintain the "hotness" that was so crucial in the new Las Vegas's success. At first, that seemed easy. As visitation increased, we threw money at the problem, built like crazy, and people came essentially to see what we were up to.

That has worked of late, but it is not a long-term strategy. Our competitors, cities such as Orlando, Florida, marvel at our success, but see it as some kind of magic. They cannot figure out how we stay on top.

It's not magic at all. What appears to be random on the surface is actually forcefully calculated decision-making aimed not only at the present, but also at the future.

That's what makes the Las Vegas Convention and Visitors Authority's decision to invest $737 million in upgrading the Las Vegas Convention Center so important. We have killed the competition in this market. When Orlando planned to expand its convention center last year, critics there rightly pointed out that this rapidly growing city, replete with Disney World, could not compete with Las Vegas for convention business.

Staying ahead of the game is neither easy nor cheap, but it is essential. It takes money to make money, something LVCVA's managing board understands. The $7.6 billion that conventioneers spent in Las Vegas last year is sure to grow.

This kind of investment keeps Las Vegas unique. It is another one of the many decisions that helps Las Vegas defy conventional economic logic. Our success is not magic at all. It is planning, forethought, and recognition that change will happen, and we need to anticipate it. Instead of resting on our laurels, we're planning what comes next. As long as that continues, Las Vegas is likely to stay on top.

February 19, 2006
Las Vegas Sun

31

There's No Slam Dunk

in Las Vegas

LAS VEGAS MAYOR OSCAR GOODMAN stole the show at last week's NBA All-Star weekend, but my guess is that all his efforts got us no closer to having a major sports team in Las Vegas.

Goodman is right: a major league baseball, basketball, or football team would be the icing on the local and regional cake, proof positive that Las Vegas has truly arrived.

But I don't think that NBA Commissioner David Stern will relent anytime soon. While Goodman and Stern have a much closer relationship than ever before, a lot of risks remain for both sides.

The hardest thing for a professional sports league is to be the first to locate in Las Vegas. Although they all point to sports betting as they demure, the reasons are more complicated.

Locating here breaks a taboo, and professional sports organizations are not generally the most creative or willing to take risks. Professional sports leagues are small clubs, and it takes rare mavericks to change the culture of such organizations.

The NBA has people who could do that, Dallas Mavericks owner Mark Cuban and Sacramento Kings owner George Maloof, prominent among them. But lacking personalities such as the acerbic Oakland Raiders owner Al Davis or the megalomaniacal Indianapolis Colts owner Robert Irsay—the two owners who nearly overturned the status quo in the NFL in the 1980s—the necessary groundswell is unlikely. Television money makes people conservative. Risk is one thing—incredibly expensive and foolish risk quite another.

NBA basketball is not a great fit for Las Vegas. This is a basketball town, true, but the distractions here, and the urgency about them, diminish every other party town in the United States. Ever wonder why New Orleans, the "city that care forgot, where everybody parties a lot," never won a title in any sport?

The NBA is a styler's league, populated by immature and callow youngsters who embrace excess as a way of life. It's barely about basketball anymore—flash and show dominate. They may love the game, but they love the nightlife considerably more.

Any owner who placed a team here would be running unusual risks. In Las Vegas, the only restraint comes from within. These days, few NBA players demonstrate that ability.

It would only be a matter of time until a video of somebody's $50 million investment stumbling out of a strip club at 9:00 a.m. on game day hit the five o'clock news. When that happened, it would confirm every bad stereotype about Las Vegas . . . and the NBA.

For Las Vegas, the risks are equally great. I have said it before and I will say it again: visitors will not fill the seats for a Las Vegas team. The premium on any individual NBA or Major League Baseball game— hockey doesn't count and the NFL is another story—simply isn't great enough to bring visitors to town, much less to the stadium.

And what stadium? Even though the WNBA has a team located in a casino in Connecticut, the NBA simply would not allow that. The Thomas & Mack Center does not have forty-one dates to give, and there are no other venues outside casinos that the NBA would deem worthy.

Public financing for an arena is out of the question. Senator Bob Beers, R-Las Vegas, would see to that. Las Vegas could not afford the half-billion dollars such an arena would cost, and in this day and age, no owner moves his team without sugar from the new location.

Even though greater Las Vegas is now big enough to support a team, it would still be a hard sell. A team needs more than eighteen thousand fans a night. The town only backs winners.

To become an entertainment option of choice, a Las Vegas franchise must win often and with panache. The city is so new that people here retain their hometown alliances. Converting them takes more than bling—it requires hardware, championship trophies. This is a front-runner's town.

If a team lands here, I will be first in line for season tickets. But even hooking the NBA All-Star game in 2007 does not give me much hope. The NFL can ignore Las Vegas, but the NBA, with its emphasis on cool, cannot.

From the NBA's point of view, the All-Star game is perfect. It satisfies its constituencies, maintains the league's complicated dance with street culture, and promises exactly nothing. David Stern would not have it any other way.

February 26, 2006
Las Vegas Sun

32

Flying to Las Vegas

WE'VE HAD IT EASY. Getting people to Las Vegas has never been the challenge that it will become.

Our popularity is a strange kind of double-edged sword, one that requires a special vigilance from the people who run our transportation systems. The success of our advertising and the special cachet of Las Vegas in postindustrial America mean that more people want to come here every year. Getting them here with ease is very likely to become the next big issue, the threat to our continued success.

Now that everyone wants to visit Las Vegas, something will have to give. We have long taken for granted that anyone who wants to come here can fly or drive in with relative ease. The incredible growth in visitation has made that a dangerous conceit, one that could cost us our lead over considerably lesser attractions.

One of the two most successful entities at handling increasing demand in the Las Vegas Valley is McCarran International Airport. Clark County Director of Aviation Randall Walker once said that he did not want the airport to become a bottleneck that stymied growth and, by and large, he has succeeded. Despite occasional backlogs at security and check-in and increasingly frequent long waits in the baggage claim, the airport works well most of the time.

The proof is in the phenomenal growth in passengers. In 2005 more than 44 million people came through McCarran, up from 36.3 million people who used the airport in 2003. The airport's capacity has long been projected to be about 50 million people per annum. If we increase at the same numeric rate during the next two years as we have in the last two, we will exceed that number.

There are certainly ways to expand the airport's capacity, and I have every expectation that airport officials will find them. But increasingly, it looks as if the projections for the opening of the new airport at Ivanpah may very well be too late. The year 2017 is the most common time frame bandied about. What happens in the meantime remains to be seen.

It won't be the outrageously high gas prices that cuts down the number of drivers who come to Las Vegas every weekend. Interstate 15 has been a nightmare for a long time, but we rarely suffer from it locally. Every Friday, long lines of traffic stream toward us from southern California. Every Sunday, longer lines return to greater Los Angeles. Las Vegans are typically headed the opposite direction, mostly with wry smiles on our faces.

Some call the 275-mile stretch "the world's largest parking lot." We hear apocryphal stories of ten-hour trips and the heartrending tales of needless fatalities abound. Every one of us marvels that people actually endure this, but we rarely ask why they do.

Even anticipating such an ordeal would take the luster off a Las Vegas weekend for me or at least make me turn in to the first Indian casino I passed on my way in on a Friday.

Las Vegas and Nevada have long had an investment in California's stretch of I-15. In the late 1990s, the Nevada Department of Transportation gave California a $10 million contribution to the road-widening project between Victorville and Barstow, and the Nevada and California congressional delegations cooperated to allow $24 million of Nevada's annual $190 million in federal road money to be spent in California as Las Vegans sat miserably in traffic.

But it has not been enough. All that money and the traffic is no better. If the airport gums up as well, we could have problems.

People on vacation don't want to spend it in the airport or on I-15, especially if they only have the weekend. Imagine yourself six hours in traffic on the way to Las Vegas and passing a sign on the side of the road that said "if you just want to gamble, you're through with your trip" or some other version of the signs that dot American highways that say "if you lived here, you'd be home by now."

If you were sick enough of the traffic and the trip, an Indian casino somewhere in the Mojave Desert might just do the trick. We should all heed the prospect.

March 5, 2006
Las Vegas Sun

33

Apathy and the Electorate

NEVADA'S POLITICS WOULD EMBARRASS any self-respecting banana republic, and the news this past week only confirms what we all know: the many fine people in Nevada politics hide a wide and shameless category who use elected office to feather their own nests.

Clark County Recorder Fran Deane is only the latest. With the G-String trials of Dario Herrera and Mary Kincaid-Chauncey beginning, Kathy Augustine, the impeached state controller, claiming vindication and planning to run for higher office, and the array of ethics complaints of all kinds against all kinds of politicians, I want to know why we put up with this. Don't these people have the decency to resign?

Our problem is part apathy and part low expectations. In Nevada, the veneer of civilization is stripped off and everybody's motives are crystal clear. We all know what that motivation is. Money matters in Las Vegas and Nevada, and that is fine in business. It works less well in politics.

Apathy is a driving force in Nevada politics. Most people simply do not care. As a result, they do not invest themselves in the political process as readily. For political leaders, this poses a dilemma. What can you do when half your district was not there the last time you ran for office?

People are engaged by issues close to home. Roads and schools bring newcomers out in droves, but airplanes flying over the neighborhood really gets them riled up. They are afraid that government is out to do them in.

Taxes are the other thing that brings the public to the ballot box. Everybody wants services, but they always want someone else to pay for them. This is an easy sell for unscrupulous politicians who want to get elected and do not care what they say to get into office. There are genuine critics of the tax structure out there—Bob Beers leading the pack—but they are in the minority.

Our expectations of political leaders are unbelievably low. Prospective jurors for the G-String trial expressed outright contempt for local political officials. From the point of view of a randomly selected group of Clark County residents, politicians were even more venal than lawyers.

The parochial expectations of the public are an enormous part of the reason why government fails us. In our time, people are fundamentally self-interested and they refuse to see beyond their own needs.

Pandering to a constituency is easy. All you have to do is tell them what they want to hear—and hope that they do not remember what you promised them six months later. Most of the time, this works. The public does not hold elected officials accountable for their promises and often not even for their behavior.

We do not expect much out of political leaders because Nevada was not set up for government to be an effective entity. In the 1960s a book called *The Great Rotten Borough* laid bare the history of Nevada politics. It is frightening that we have changed so little even as the stakes here have risen and the state has been transformed from a bit player in the United States to a central position in culture and economics.

There are plenty of good and decent people in Nevada politics, but by implication, the sleaze factor drags down the good ones. Thomas Jefferson once said, "Eternal vigilance is the price of liberty." In Nevada, we have simply not been vigilant enough. We have not insisted on our "liberty," as Jefferson would have seen it, nor have we demanded responsive government.

On the slate this year, the good candidates—the ones who believe in something, whether I agree with it or not, and the ones who see government as an instrument of the people—may very well outnumber the sleazeballs. It is up to the people to make sure that our elected leaders reflect our hopes and not our fears.

If we are lucky, we will get better government, but only if the public insists and forcefully implements that demand. It will help if the public pays more attention, gets beyond knee-jerk reactions, and demands elected officials who believe in something other than lining their own pockets. It will not be easy, but we can get there. And we will have a better Nevada when we do.

March 19, 2006
Las Vegas Sun

34

Gaming and Technology

A FRIEND OF MINE, a quintessential old Las Vegas gal, was bemoaning the changes in the city, but not in the usual way. Instead of complaining about the size of the hotels or the lack of comps like so many do, she focused on the casino floor.

"I remember rows and rows of tables, with people laughing, talking, engaged with each other," she wistfully recalled. "Now, it is machines, one-armed bandits are everywhere, and nobody talks. They just don't look like they are having fun."

Now, I dearly love my friend, but the way I see it, the only good thing about the good old days is bad memory. There is something in what she said, no doubt, but reality is a lot more complicated.

I see people having fun at the tables, but they are usually younger, out for a night on the town. They travel in packs—I think they call them "posses" now—and slap hands and hoot and holler. The people at the machines are generally older, more solitary, and certainly less inclined to jump up and down.

But my friend had a point. If you had told someone in 1975 that the legalization of gaming in Atlantic City, the spread of Indian gaming, and the entire array of Internet and online options to wager would have improved Las Vegas's position in the gaming universe, they would have thought you were nuts.

So gaming has changed in the past thirty years, both in where you can play and in the nature of the play. It's worth thinking about how it might change in the next decade.

Imagine being able to play 21 on your cell phone as you waited for the dentist. Realistically, you can buy such a program and install it yourself already. You just can't win money.

Especially for younger consumers—the ones who shout out their victories on the casino floor—this kind of delivery is natural. They have grown up in a twelve-images-a-second world, accustomed to never having a down moment. No pause is too brief to fill with another activity. I don't quite get it, but I doubt I am supposed to.

So we are in the classic American situation: technology has once again outstripped law, creating possibilities that the lawmakers who created Nevada's gaming statutes never envisioned.

Las Vegas remains secure to date, the place where the twenty-somethings come to show they are real. While we are on top because of our entertainment, we have not yet considered how to approach the technologically sophisticated daily gaming market. It is money on the table for us, and I for one hate to see it left sitting there.

Don't get me wrong. Bricks and mortar casinos are not going anywhere. But what seems to be happening is that they are becoming increasingly ancillary to the larger entertainment picture. Still the largest piece of the Las Vegas visitor expenditure, gaming is diminishing as a share of the whole, even as the dollar numbers continue to rise.

The next decade may very well challenge our assumptions about the delivery of gaming.

It is hard to imagine that Nevada will willingly cede this piece of a growing and lucrative market to offshore online gamers. Our special trait has been flexibility, response to new stimuli in the market. That's how we have succeeded to date.

With all the changes in the delivery of information, the only thing stopping you from gambling on your cell phone is law; we all know that the law is mutable, changed at the discretion of the legislature. Given the real challenge from Internet gaming, the prospect of a change in Nevada law to accommodate direct delivery of legalized gaming is not as farfetched as it sounds.

May 21, 2006
Las Vegas Sun

35

A Scandalous Past

THE BROUHAHA THAT THE *Los Angeles Times* ignited in our judiciary is another piece of evidence in the long chain that shows Las Vegas and southern Nevada are not quite there yet.

I guess I am not surprised, but I am a little disappointed. On the heels of the G-String case, the idea that business as usual among public officials and the constituencies they serve continues unabated is galling.

And then Justice of the Peace Karen Bennett-Haron has the audacity to arbitrarily grant a three-day reprieve from arrest for the beleaguered Fran Deane, who was not even in the courtroom! Sheriff Bill Young was not the only person who was outraged by this capricious decision. If the law applies to one, it should apply to all.

Don't these people read the papers? Or are they so smug that they don't care?

Maybe they know more than the rest of us. The default in Nevada politics since statehood has been centralized power that runs the state for its own benefit. An ordinary citizen could not catch a break. First it was the Comstock, where the U.S. senators were part of the crew that dominated mining. After the demise of mining, the railroad ran the state. After that, a hardscrabble saloonkeeper turned magnate named George Wingfield owned the state for the better part of thirty years. Since then, it has been gaming and most recently real estate developers have challenged for a seat at the table.

With such a tawdry history, I suppose that it would be too much to expect judges to decline money from the attorneys who bring cases before them or to handle a nearly defrocked public official the way they do the rest of us.

But the pattern is old and established. Grease turns the wheels, in this case of justice.

The issue has little to do with whether judges are elected or appointed. We know that elections, at least for the judiciary, have real flaws; a case can be made that appointment would yield its own level of cronyism. Our problems run much deeper.

We have to address the parochial nature of local politics. Even though greater Las Vegas has become a community of nearly 2 million people, in too many areas our institutions have not grown up with the city. Obviously, some elected officials behave as though public office is a license to loot.

The judiciary is captive to the very industry it regulates, and it takes an out-of-town newspaper to alert us. Folks, that does not meet my definition of grown-up politics.

The problem is growing. We continue to allow a cozy and even incestuous relationship between elected power and the business community. While former Municipal Judge Dayvid Figler believes that little will change because Nevada law allows judges so much discretion, it is time that such power is curtailed.

The test should be simple for everyone in public office: If it looks like a duck and smells like a duck, it is a duck. Even the appearance of conflict of interest or impropriety should be a red flag for anyone who faces election or seeks appointment.

If it looks bad on the 5:00 p.m. news and you do it, you should be unfit for office not only in Las Vegas, but also in Nevada as a whole. If we are to build a state worthy of the name—and neither the *New York Times* nor the *Los Angeles Times* would give us our due at this time—it requires much tighter regulation of the relationship between not only the judiciary, but also all public officials, and the communities they ostensibly serve.

The reasons for this change are as much about preserving the quality of life in Nevada as they are about any abstract sense of morality. As more companies come to do business here and new residents abound, they have a reasonable expectation of being treated fairly.

Exposés such as the one in the *Los Angeles Times* hurt us in more than visible ways. They suggest that Nevada remains the "great rotten borough" of legend, a place where you might not want to invest your money.

Even in the middle of a $20 billion construction boom, we have to look to the future. Tamping down on the good ole boy idiosyncrasies of our ribald past is as good a place as any to start.

June 18, 2006
Las Vegas Sun

36

Follow the Governor's Money

NEVADA INVERTS the old journalistic adage to follow the money. When people say this, they usually follow where the money goes. In Nevada, you get to the truth faster if you see where the money comes from.

For the last decade, we have assumed that *Las Vegas Sun* columnist Jon Ralston has correctly described our gubernatorial elections as "anointments." He has argued that we don't really elect our leaders; instead, a backroom cabal of powerful interests that run the state choose for us and seed the process with so much money—which translates into TV commercials, the only way most of us can tell the candidates apart—that the result is foreordained.

The Abramoff-DeLay scandal has made the American public even more wary of the effect money has on politics. If we didn't already think special interests owned our politicians, Abramoff's manipulation of the system is enough to make anyone a cynic.

Jim Gibbons's, the presumptive front-runner in this year's governor's race, is almost glib about financial disclosure. "It is Jim Gibbons' belief that voters should be able to see who is funding each candidate's campaign before voting," Gibbon's campaign manager Robert Uithoven told the Associated Press. Gibbons wants you to know who supports him; I want you to think about what it means.

Gibbons's financial disclosure form gives us a heads up about where the power will lie if he is elected. According to AP, Gibbons has amassed $4 million. Included in that amount is $317,000 carried over from his congressional war chest, and $1.7 million that he has raised since the last reporting period.

Gibbons's support comes from a wide base in state business. Twenty percent has come from the gaming and leisure industry, 17 percent from development and construction, and 15 percent from physicians and pharmaceutical companies. The mining industry gave him a paltry $12,000, and a number of prominent individuals, including media mogul and university system Chancellor Jim Rogers and northern Nevada developer and brothel owner Lance Gilman, gave $5,000 apiece.

What does this mean for you and me? For much of the past decade, job growth in the gaming and leisure industry has not been as rapid as in other employment sectors. In Clark County, we have seen employment become more diverse, with an ever-smaller percentage of workers in the resort corridor.

But gaming and leisure is the single biggest giver to Gibbons, a state of affairs that suggests a return to the status quo of the 1980s and 1990s. During the "Mirage Phase," between 1989 and 2000, what was good for gaming and leisure was good for the state. The industry met a sort of Waterloo in the 2003 legislative session, when its dominance of state politics was usurped by competitors. In this changing climate, gaming and leisure's generosity may portend greater influence for this sector of the economy.

The people who supplanted gaming at the table in 2003 were from development and construction. This industry is the fastest-growing in the state, and with the construction boom that is occurring in Las Vegas, its influence is likely to continue to expand. Congressman Gibbons may be disappointed at the comparatively parsimonious giving of this sector.

The doctors and the pharmaceutical companies seem better organized and more generous this year than in the past. Both have real issues to bring before state government. Remember the commercials where doctors walked past the sign for the Nevada state line? Nevada's physicians have seen their malpractice rates soar and they may feel they need a friend in the statehouse.

The pharmaceutical industry has its own objective. As of July 1, Nevada residents can buy drugs from Canadian pharmacies.

Pharmaceutical companies may plan an assault on this law; they may simply be investing as a way to cut their losses.

Mining, essentially a parasite in the state, only gave $12,000. Maybe the mining industry, which statewide employed 11,690 people in 2004, the equivalent of one major hotel-casino, feels like its prior relationship with Gibbons, who represented mining as a congressman, will sustain it. For an industry with amazing profits that paid only $39 million in mineral taxes in 2004 and had little effect on the state economy as a whole, this smacks of arrogance.

So looking at where the money comes from tells you a lot about what Jim Gibbons will do as governor. The question is: do you like this picture?

August 6, 2006
Las Vegas Sun

37

Groping Governor?

I DOUBT WE WILL EVER REALLY KNOW what happened between Jim Gibbons and Chrissy Mazzeo in the parking garage on a rainy Friday night. The hubbub has been great, as befits a possible scandal involving the presumptive heir to the throne of Nevada, the governorship.

Most amazing about the situation is that Gibbons has based his run on character issues. He has said time and again that he is the most qualified to hold the highest office in the state because of what he has learned in his many roles. Even in the most recent gubernatorial faux debate, and I say that because the candidates don't really get to debate one another, Gibbons trotted out his résumé as a closing argument. He told the public that we could trust his judgment and that was reason enough to vote for him.

In vino veritas, the saying goes. But in wine is also trouble and confusion. It is hard to blame a guy for sitting out a rainstorm with a glass of wine or two, but from that point on, Gibbons's judgment, the very characteristic he touts as his primary qualification for the office he seeks, comes into serious question.

In our day, public life can only be lived by one standard: how would any behavior look on the evening news? Where there is smoke, there is fire, a distrustful public is bound to think, along with the truly danger-ous supposition for Gibbons: is he really who he says he is?

Gibbons's biggest problem is that while he can rightly claim that he represents all seventeen counties in Nevada, he only has a sliver of the most important. Clark County has two other congressional representatives. Most of us simply don't know Gibbons very well. And when two-thirds of the voting public barely knows your name, drinking with strangers isn't the fastest way to have them see you in a positive light.

Worse for the candidate, his response smacks of the capricious use of power. Despite überconsultant and political kingmaker par excellence Sig Rogich's assertion that Mazzeo recanted her charges, the police report indicates that she didn't want to face off against the mass of power Gibbons had at his fingertips.

You can't lay that decision off on him, but she clearly miscalculated. Gibbons's news conference Thursday afternoon demonstrated how uninspired and inept the man and his campaign are. I was stunned at the weak response that brought nothing of substance to the situation.

Even more, Gibbons runs the risk of being tarred by the Foley brush. Another Republican congressman has behaved badly or at least given the appearance of doing so. It may try the patience of an already skeptical public. Again this comes back to the congressman's self-proclaimed strength and new Achilles' heel, his judgment.

I can't tell whether Gibbons will survive this incident. His campaign can only be described as lackluster, and I am afraid that is a generous assessment. There is no good response to such charges in postmodern America. An older America reserved the libel suit for those who felt unjustly accused of something that damaged their public standing, but those days are forever gone. Besides, who could Gibbons sue? No one has filed charges against him or otherwise done anything to him since the evening's fateful events, whatever they were, transpired.

Gibbons is in the unenviable position of having friends, who are trying to exonerate him from negative public perception, keeping the story alive. With friends like these, who needs to stop in the bar for a drink?

In the end, this is a garden variety scandal that happened at a particularly inopportune moment to a candidate who had been coasting since the race began. Whether injustice personified or accurate characterization, it challenges a candidate who had seen fit to run on his personal traits, not his legislative accomplishments or his plans for the future of the state. Those who live by character issues in politics alone always run the risk of being bitten. Public opinion is always fickle and it loves even a whiff of scandal. Jim Gibbons inadvertently gave the public that when he ducked in out of the rain.

October 22, 2006
Las Vegas Sun

Desert, southwestern edge. Photo by Virgil Hancock III.

Part III
The Western Environment

Introduction

Goodbye Preservation, Hello Recreation

IN THE AMERICAN WEST the age of preservation has ended and that of recreation has begun.

Preservation is predicated on what is now a more than century-old, class-based value system. It began as conservation in the age of Theodore Roosevelt, when it was easy to separate sacred space and that fouled by humans, and even easier for those who fouled that space to accept the distinction and throw their energy into preserving places that were beautiful and remote. No wonder conservation and preservation were watchwords of the American elite for the first half of the twentieth century and beyond.

These values turned into environmentalism, a heady set of ideas during the 1960s and 1970s, when Americans embraced a vision of the world that was frankly complacent and just a little bit flushed with its own affluence. Environmentalism placed an incredibly high premium on the idea of wilderness, tacitly implying that prosperity had created a world in which all who deserved affluence had attained it. At the end of the American industrial economy, this premise led to great pressure to add existing wilderness.

These principles have now grown stale and even archaic. Environmentalism is a set of values, not the Ten Commandments. As a value system, it has to compete for adherents.

In the 1960s and 1970s, its version of authenticity held center stage. Of late, it hasn't.

It's not that young people today don't understand what these values are; they do. What they don't understand is why these values are better than what they think is important. Today's young people have a different idea of what is authentic. They are postliterate, twelve-images-per-second beings. The IMAX in high definition gives a better view than anything they can do themselves. And they don't have to get cold or wet. From the point of view of an awful lot of young people today, why not? Why endure when technology can provide a visually better experience without the discomfort?

This is a profound and remarkable change that substantially alters the physical and psychic landscape of the American West. It means, among other things, that recreationalists, motorized and otherwise, have won. Wilderness is dead; not as reserved land, but as a movement or a viable political strategy. Its constituency is aging and it is losing political support to recreation by leaps and bounds.

As a result of political change, wilderness advocates can no longer get a hearing; twenty years ago, they simply swaggered to the table, pulled out maps and the rulebook they'd written, and achieved results.

Now they are supplicants, coming hat in hand, pleading their case, and threatening legal action. As annoying as federal agencies may find lawsuits, they're evidence of a loss of political power and support. In the 1980s, public outcry overturned Secretary of the Interior James Watt's administrative reforms of policy; Watt himself was ousted. Today, advocates resort to threats and the figurative bomb blast of a lawsuit. What is this, Guatemala? In the United States, throwing bombs, real or otherwise, reveals a lack of power.

Recreationalists have become the new conservationists, and with that comes a great deal more responsibility than the recreational community has ever before assumed. Having easily juxtapositioned themselves as victims of the excesses of wilderness advocates, recreationalists of all kinds must now assume the onus of power.

This is especially true for motorized recreation, the fastest-growing dimension of the outdoor world. Recreationalists prize scenery, beauty, and the challenge of the outdoors; they just tend to do so more and more with technology. In this they are no different than the rest of us. We all use technology, cell phones, iPods, and everything else to make our lives easier and more pleasurable. Since Gore-Tex, recreationalists have done the same thing. The capability of technology has grown immensely, effectively allowing the forty-seven-year-old me to do things now that I could not do on my own in my twenties.

So now, the shift begins. As all forms of technology allow people deeper and deeper into the backcountry and as wilderness advocacy goes by the wayside in a postindustrial society, recreationalists will have to police themselves. Instead of trying to push the frontiers of what they can do and how they can do it, in their own self-interest, they will have to find ways to put boundaries around the resources they treasure, so those resources will be preserved for their future use.

It is a paradoxical situation: the outsiders have become kings and queens of the castle. It is a whole lot easier to sit outside the tent and throw firecrackers inside; it is much, much harder to sit inside the tent and govern not only your enemies, but your close friends as well.

No longer do recreationalists grapple with opponents about which lands they can use. The entire recreational community must now develop an ethic of sustainability that will assure that what the sports recreationalists choose continues for generations. Leadership that provides stewardship of the resources it uses and consumes and develops a political position that wisely manages power from the inside rather than sits outside carping is essential. Recreation now faces an internal struggle among its many constituencies to define its values, the dos and don'ts of a new land ethic.

It is a sea change in the American West, a reorganization of how we as a culture have approached the outdoors for the better part of four decades. It requires that those of us who love the American West find new ways to communicate with one another to preserve as much of it as we can, for use as well as for its own sake.

January 15, 2006
Newwest.org

38

The Perils of Ecotourism

EACH WINTER, THE HUMPBACK WHALES arrive in Lahaina harbor off the island of Maui in search of warmer waters in which to breed as airplanes disgorge untold winter visitors to the islands. The whales have come since time immemorial, appearing in Hawaiian legend and the earliest Anglo American accounts, gracing the art and cultural imagery of the Hawaiian islands; the tourists have come in numbers only since the end of World War II. The whales have great symbolic power, investing legend and fiction with meaning for as long as humans have had contact with the species. In recent years, they have become the focus of protective legislation, with fines now levied even for coming too close to these stunning creatures as they cavort in the sea and engage in their mating ritual. They have also become an attraction for visitors to the island, who buy tickets aboard all manner of seacraft, from large sloops to the fourteen-foot Zodiac pontoon raft my wife and I boarded, in an effort to photograph or even catch a glimpse of these spectacular and now very rare mammals. As the boat sped out into the water, I watched my fellow tourists as much as I watched the water. Cameras in hand, we all sought to capture an image of these beings, as if our interest alone will be sufficient to preserve a species decimated by more than 150 years of commercial hunting.

Once, Lahaina harbor sheltered other forms of commerce. Two commodities dominated the middle nineteenth century, the trade in souls converted by the God-fearing Protestant missionaries who first descended upon Hawaii during the 1820s and the rest and revelry that was a byproduct of the commerce in the meat, fat, oil, and skin that came from the whales that sheltered there in the winter. These two outside cultural and economic forms pressed against each other, squeezing Hawaiians between them. The missionaries sought to convert Hawaiian souls en masse; the whalers experienced better success enjoying the spoils of the whales they slaughtered throughout the northern Pacific Ocean. No legislation or moralizing sermon saved these ocean creatures. Only the replacement of whale oil with petroleum products prevented the extinction of the magnificent species that wintered in the Hawaiian islands.

We, as modern tourists, revel in the viewing of the whales, in the act of communing with what we see as pure nature. We become ecotourists when we watch the whales, people who share in an experience that we define as pleasurable. If we choose, we can easily make this watching a social good. The often outrageous sums such voyaging costs we interpret as a part of the process of saving the planet for future generations; by investing in an experience we can only see, not take home with us, we give the whales and other endangered species a place in the human future. We go to see and not harpoon these magnificent creatures, a situation we purposefully read as evidence of the spread of the liberal value system of the industrial world. Our ancestors used their power to kill these fabulous mammals; our actions let us believe we are better because we choose to protect and appreciate them. There is a certainty born of arrogance and too much money entwined with wonder in many of the tourists who disembark like I did, bandy-legged and sunburned, from watercraft after an afternoon's whale-watching.

The view of the whales obscures a more complicated reality on Maui. Caught by the prism of our interest, we play the lead role within a script written to affirm our choices as we searched for dolphins beneath the blue-green waters on our way back to shore. We become mesmerized by our own presence in the scene our culture and imagination constructs. We play the roles in the script as if they are real; lulled, we fail to see and understand the industrial and postindustrial worlds that grant this pleasure and give meaning to this ritual, blissfully regarding our self-defined enlightened behavior as a natural result of human endeavor rather than a commercial process of creating and consuming commodities in its own right.

As I turned to look at the shore from the water, I saw in full bloom the complicated structures and processes of modern tourism. The shoreline reveals an economic and cultural geography of tourism, a process of designing and defining intangible commodities that can be psychologically possessed through spending. If in the Southwest, as the writer Ross Calvin once suggested, sky determines, on Maui, elevation determines. Along the shoreline sprawl the communities of Kaanapali and Lahaina, dominated by the many shops, luxury hotels, restaurants, and other amenities essential to support modern tourists, far from home, as they experience the islands. Here is a world visitors comprehend. It refracts them to themselves; they see it on their own terms.

Above this plane, but intimately tied to it are the sugarcane fields, waving in the breeze as workers cut the silver-green stalks. Proximate to the tourist amenities, the cane fields so essential in the history of Hawaii show the tentacles of tourism creeping upon them; through the adjacent fields chugs the Sugarcane Train, replete with its singing conductor, Glen Foster, who cheerily crooned an odd combination of nostalgic mainland melodies, "Oh Susannah" and "Sweet Betsy From Pike," and Hawaiian work songs, as we rode along, looking at the incongruous sights. The train pulled us on a one-hour tour amid sweating laborers hard at work in the fields. The songs, the ambience, the frivolity of the ride tell a story of this space that is about the visitor and not the fields; the ambience pulls tourists' attention from the physical labor of reality to the scenic sights and stories of mythic Maui. Most of the tourists look at the harbor, the hotels, the golf courses, and the sea, and when they see the labor around them, it is exotic or romantic rather than essential, sweaty, or backbreaking. Looking too closely at the workers themselves seemed dislocating, anachronistic, out of place in this carefully scripted scene.

Above the cane fields, a romantic mise-en-scène, cattle roam the sides of the hills farther from town but still distinctly visible from the sea. Herdsmen round up animals for branding and castrating in the cool of the hillsides, away from the salt air and humidity of the lower elevations. Once part of the empires of great barons, the cattle are now an anachronism, an important economic activity to specific families, but far less important in the shape of the island economy. Yet romance remains in this action, a feeling of human endeavor in a lush environment in a simpler time, a constructed meaning for observers who seek a mythological Hawaii they can fathom and a livelihood for those few fortunate enough to retain employment in the industry.

At the highest elevations, the volcanoes beckon to visitors, and the steady stream of automobiles on the narrow roads to the top of volcanic craters again attests to the reemergence of the visitor-based economy amid the clouds that shroud Maui's mountain peaks. Restaurants dot the sides of the roads along the elevated climb, and the complexion of the people we passed changed from the bronze, brown, and golden hues of cane workers and cowboys to the alabaster and sunburned red of visitors like us. In the thin air at these pinnacles, visitors feel intimidated. The power of the volcano saps our confidence, challenges our illusion of control. Only the road tells us we remain powerful and important, in tune with nature, and part of a culture that successfully subjugated these places. This is the tourist's illusion, a way of seeing that comes from brief jaunts to faraway places and guidebooks instead of venturing beyond convenience.

The geography of tourism illustrates the economic history of the island. There is a linear progression of activities in Maui's history, a series of colonial processes that show their skeletons along the shoreline, impressing a complex network of relationships atop existing local norms. Whaling came first, and Lahaina testifies to it. Sugar and cattle followed, both raw materials exported to the mainland in classic colonial fashion. Tourism followed, capping and underpinning other economic forms. Its geography is logical, predictable, and organized, from beaches to golf courses to volcanic national parks; it is a template placed upon, or perhaps over, local life and local ways, one that has become the prism through which the world sees Maui.

As in Maui, tourism is a devil's bargain, but this is true throughout the nation and the world. Despite its reputation as a panacea for the economic ills of places that have lost their way in the postindustrial world or for those that never previously found it, tourism typically fails to meet the expectations of communities and regions that embrace it as an economic strategy. Regions, communities, and locales welcome tourism as an economic boon, only to find that it irrevocably changes them in unanticipated and uncontrollable ways. From this one enormous devil's bargain, the dilemma of a panacea that cannot fulfill its promise and alters instead of fixes, flows an entire collection of closely related conditions that complement the process of change in overt and subtle ways. Tourism transforms culture, making it into something new and foreign; it may or may not rescue economies. As a viable option for moribund or declining places, tourism promises much but delivers only a little, often in different forms and ways than its advocates anticipate. Its local beneficiaries come from a small segment of the population, "the growth coalition," the landowners, developers, planners, builders, real estate sales and management interests, bankers, brokers, and others. The capital that sustains these interests comes from elsewhere, changing local relationships and the values that underpin them, along with their vision of place. Others flounder, finding their land their greatest asset and their labor lightly valued. With tourism comes unanticipated and irreversible consequences, unexpected and unintended social, cultural, economic, demographic, environmental, and political consequences that communities, their leaders, and their residents typically face unprepared.

The embrace of tourism triggers an all-encompassing contest for the soul of a place, a battle for the meaning of local identity. Identity depends on the context of the place—is linked to its social shape as well as its economy, environment, and culture—and challenges to it threaten the status quo, especially when they pull on the bonds of community by pitting different elements that shared previous alliances against one another. As these bonds fray, sub rosa tension—there all the time but buried in the fictions of social arrangements—comes to the surface as the impact of change throws the soul of the place, any place, up for grabs.

Throughout the world, tourism initiates this contest as it regenerates myriad patterns that challenge the existing structure of communities and reshapes them. The initial development of tourism often seems innocuous and harmless, "beneath the radar" of outside interests, lucrative but not transformative. As places acquire the cachet of desirability with travelers, they draw people and money; the redistribution of wealth, power, and status follow, complicating local arrangements. When tourism creates sufficient wealth, it becomes too important to be left to the locals. Power moves away from local decision-makers, even those who psychically and socially invest in the ways of the new system tourism creates, and toward outside capital and its local representatives. This redistribution changes internal relations as over time it consolidates into a new dominant template or overlay for the places it develops. The new shape disenfranchises most locals as it makes some natives and most "neonatives"—those who are attracted to the places that have become tourist towns by the traits of the transformed place—economically better off and creates a place that becomes a mirror image of itself as its identity is marketed. A series of characteristic and oft repeated consequences results from this scenario, leaving all but a few in tourist communities questioning whether they were better off in the economic doldrums in which they lived before tourism came to town.

In this sense, tourism is the most colonial of colonial economies, not because of the sheer physical difficulty or the pain or humiliation intrinsic in its labor, but as a result of its psychic and social impact on people and their places. Tourism and the social structure it provides makes unknowing locals into people who look like themselves but who act and believe differently as they learn to market their place and its, and their, identity. They change every bit as much as did African workers in the copper mines of the Congo or the diamond mines of South Africa, men from rural homelands who became industrial cannon fodder. Unlike laborers in these colonial enterprises, who lived in obscurity as they labored, tourist workers face an enormous contradiction: who and what they are is crucial to visitors in the abstract; who they are as service workers is entirely meaningless. Tourist workers quickly learn that one of the most essential traits of tourist service is to mirror onto the guest what that visitor wants from you and your place in a way that affirms the visitor's self-image.

Here begins a dilemma, a place where locals must be what visitors want them to be in order to feed and clothe themselves and their families, but also must guard themselves, their soul, and their place, from those who less appreciate its special traits. They negotiate these boundaries, creating a series of "boxes" between themselves and visitors, rooms in which locals encourage visitors to feel that they have become of the place but where these locals also subtly guide visitors away from the essence of being local. The Sugarcane Train in Maui nods in this direction as the conductor tells us his story; tourists do not much care about the stories of the cane-cutters outside the train window. In this process, the visited become something else, somehow different from who they were before as they exchange the privilege of their identity. This offer to share an image of their sense of belonging for coin becomes a far more comprehensive and often more perplexing bargain than merely exchanging labor and the assets in their ground or on it for their sustenance.

This process of scripting space, both physically and psychically, defines tourist towns and resorts. All places have scripted space; the scripting of space is part and parcel of the organizing of the physical and social world for the purpose of perpetuation. Like commercial space, tourist space is specially scripted to keep the visitor at the center of the picture while simultaneously cloaking, manipulating, and even deceiving them into believing that their experience is the local's life, reality, and view of the world. "Wasn't it wonderful here [in Hawaii] before Captain Cook showed up," a friend said to me over dinner at an exquisite shoreside restaurant in Ma'alea Bay, Maui, thoroughly swallowing the fiction of the scripted space of tourism.

Despite often seductively quaint and romantic settings, seeming harmlessness, and a reputation as a "clean" industry, tourism is of a piece with the modern and postindustrial, postmodern worlds; its social structures and cultural ways are those of an extractive industry. While its environmental byproducts are not the tailings piles of uranium mining, in the West, they include the spread of real estate development, the gobbling up of open space in narrow mountain valleys, the traffic and sprawl of expansive suburban communities, and the transformation of the physical environment into roads and reservoirs that provide activity and convenience for visitors. Tourism offers its visitors romanticized visions of the historic past, the natural world, popular culture, and especially of themselves. The sale of these messages, even in their least trammeled form is what iconoclastic author Edward Abbey called "industrial tourism," the packaging and marketing of experience as commodity within the boundaries of the accepted level of convenience to the public.

The most postmodern of such devices, the ones that meld the technologies, attitudes, and styles of the Age of Information, the era of the global transmission of knowledge that followed 1980, go even further. They purposely create another level of experience that masquerades or prepares for so-called authentic experience, blurring any line that may remain and often making the replica more seductive than the original. Using experience to script space in another way, to design artificial controls that seem natural and ordinary as they highlight the activity by subtly persuading the visitor that the activity is their own, this postmodern form shatters historical distinctions between the real and the unreal by producing faux replicas of experience independent of the activity from which they derive.

With the varieties of experience available in the postmodern world, all tourism, from Surge Rock in Las Vegas to the Eiffel Tower to an

African safari, and even backpacking in the Bob Marshall Wilderness in Montana or following in the footsteps of protoarchaeologist Heinrich Schliemann, is scripted industrial tourism. The wealth of industrial society, its transportation technologies, its consumer goods, emphasis on convenience, and the values of a postmodern, postconsumption culture create the surplus that allows people to select any experience they choose. Its goal is not experience, but fulfillment—experience that makes the chooser feel important, strong, powerful, a member of the "right" crowd, or whatever else they crave. Those determined to leave mainstream society in search of an individual sense of nontourist travel are scripted into believing that backpacking in the Bob Marshall makes them unique or at least part of a rare breed, somehow intellectually and morally above other tourists. This conceit is common among elites—academics and environmentalists among them—who believe they know better than the rest of humanity. The embrace of the inherently fraudulent "ecotourism," a mere codeword for an activity that so parallels the colonial tourism of Theodore Roosevelt in Africa, in the hopes of creating a better world reveals a stunning naïveté. Finding the little out-of-the-way inn in rural Ireland no more "invents" a unique experience than does a bus tour of Las Vegas or the Universal Studios tour in Los Angeles. It merely offers a wrapper that promises certain sensibilities a self-affirming "authentic experience" in the viewer's terms. The delusion of distance from their society and the superiority of spirit and sometimes skill it connotes exists even for the climbers of Mount Everest. Even as Rob Hall, the vaunted New Zealander, guide of the Himalayas, recognized his death was imminent during a tragic May 1996 ascent, he spoke to his eight-months-pregnant wife and through her, his unborn child, on a satellite phone, diminishing the idea that any form of tourism can be other than that of the global market. The expedition took place so that people who could afford it could feel personally satisfied; a total of eight people died as a result. "Bagging trophy," as some caustically refer to the status side of postmodern tourism, can be dangerous as well as exhilarating.

Ecotourism as Culture: Selling Identity Along with Place

Whether in the United States or elsewhere, ecotourism makes promises to its visitors. Purveyors tell ecotourists that by engaging in this activity, they are doing a number of good things: they are protecting nature, preventing industrialization of the pristine, and promoting sustainability. Ecotourists are not "Ugly Americans," as Eugene Burdick and William Lederer coined the phrase (in another context) during the 1950s, nor are they the well-meaning but misguided colonials of Graham Greene novels. Instead, ecotourism promises, you the ecotourist help the scenario. You enter lightly, walk quietly, experience authenticity, and go on your way reinvigorated, leaving a world unchanged and undamaged as a result of your stay. You tread lightly, fulfilling the adage "leave only footprints and take only pictures."

There's a flipside to this picture. Ecotourism tells its customers that they are helping, that they are preserving crafts, maintaining the lifestyles of native peoples, and in other ways positively contributing to the preservation of the things they value. The money they spend preserves, we believe as wholly as did the whale-watchers who began this story, rather than destroys and a complicated equation, in which the buyer is persuaded that a figurative box they enter is real. They're told that the experience they're having is authentic, that local people benefit, and that the environment is protected and we want to believe it, want to feel that our experience is better than other kinds. So we don't look closely, don't peel back the layers, and go away, our smugness intact.

The truth is harder and colder: too often, the people by the side of the road selling crafts don't share in the benefits of ecotourism. They are props in a scene of fictive tranquility, one more piece of evidence in the eye of the beholder that the traveler has entered an authentic scene, quaint, charming, and undisturbed by modernity. Ecotourists tell themselves that the scenes are unchanged except by their arrival and their presence helps to preserve these glimpses of a purer past. It may be the worst story we tell ourselves, the one that lets us feel especially good about our role and frees us from the guilt of exploitation without doing a single thing for the people of the place. We buy from such vendors, we let them show us around out of a gratuitous paternalism, grateful for the opportunity to help preserve.

Local participants rarely enjoy much of the highly touted economic benefits of ecotourism. From Belize to Bangalore, locals get the crumbs and consequences. A few who had experience with the larger world prior to tourism or who quickly grasp the rhythms and tenets of the service economy may garner some personal prosperity. Most end up where they started, on the bottom of the economic scrapheap. Even wages, usually better than in subsistence agriculture or more commonly peonage, represent another of the many trade-offs.

The impact of tourism is very often the transformation of culture. In the Third World especially, ecotourism functions as does cable television: it opens the window to the First World, with all its advantages, temptations, and expectations. Usually this raises local expectations, but access to amenities almost never keeps pace. In the rare cases that it does, there are problems close at hand. Fulfilling expectations causes fundamental change. The people of a place look the same but act different. They think differently. They've acquired a new value system. They are the same physical beings when they deal with tourists, the date change from people who reflect a value system rooted in the place to ones who try to anticipate what visitors want. They learn to hold up a mirror for visitors and subtly ask how these newcomers want to see their own reflection. Then they become adept at providing affirmation of the mirror image, effectively offering up their identity for a price.

Selling identity has its pitfalls. It commodifies sentiment with experience, melding psychic and physical activities into a unit in which actions and thoughts are inextricably linked. Even in the United States, places that possess a symbolism that they share with no other part of the country, a meaning encoded in their very names, experience the same peril. Myths, stories, and tales abound; songs even carry this forward. Charlie Daniels's "Wyoming on my Mind" is about a great deal more than Wyoming as a place, more than the geography of the state, more than Wyoming's natural and social attributes. It's also the hook in the state of Wyoming's tourism promotion package.

Fixed and Malleable Identities

When people visit, they want to belong, to be of the place if not from it. That's the wrapper to the package, the real reason behind the activity that draws people West. On a horse ride to see a remote place with an Indian guide, the activity of riding, a recreational activity, is really not as important as riding *with an Indian*, as anyone who grew up in the United States knows. Riding is significant, but it is the idea of riding with an Indian that makes it special, even more special than riding with a real cowboy. This feeling, this cultural code, is why *The Brady Bunch*, the old 1970s show now back in vogue, had an episode in which the entire family was adopted into an Indian tribe, presumably the Havasupai, at the Grand Canyon. This gesture on the part of Native people made the Bradys real to themselves. They belonged; what more could an American family ask?

Ecotourism and the Future

Postmodern capitalism is new terrain, largely unrecognizable except to those who experience it. It is not the capitalism of Andrew Carnegie, J. P. Morgan, Henry Ford, Armand Hammer, or J. Paul Getty, but more that of Walt Disney, Bill Gates, and gaming impresario Steve Wynn. It is not national or nationalistic, but transnational and global. Its emphasis is not on the tangible of making things, of ever-larger assembly lines and production processes, but in the marketing of images, of information, of spectacle. It creates information and information-processing systems and the accouterments that turn regional and national economic endeavor into a global commodity. Of equal significance, postmodern, postindustrial capitalism produces images that convey emotions, hope and contentment chief among them, as well as conduits through which information can travel. It is a form at once substantial and inconsequential, crucial yet trivial, meaningful yet ephemeral. Its sociocultural impact is vast; in its ability to move information, and as a result to move more traditional forms of economic endeavor such as assembly line work, postmodern global capitalism is truly revolutionary. Postindustrial capitalism has changed the very meaning of economic endeavor, providing new ways to produce wealth in a transformation as profound as the industrial revolution.

In the postindustrial world, Americans became consumers of more than tangible goods, of the spirit and meaning of things rather than of their physical properties. What Americans of a certain class could touch and hold no longer exclusively granted the security and importance to which its possessors were accustomed; when anyone could lease a BMW, the elite needed more: the control of feelings, emotion, identity, and modes of understanding that signified status, a way to differentiate themselves from the increasingly luxurious mass cultural norm. In a world short on time, in which only the very rich and the very poor possessed it and only one of those two groups had the means to utilize it, a new way to define the self as special came to the fore. In turn, this created a new form of commodification that came to dominate the American and international landscape. Corporations packaged and people purchased what they felt granted them identity, but that identity ceased to follow traditional iconography and became a product of the international culture marketplace. Modernism had been about finding the individual's place in the world of machines; the mergers and downsizing of postindustrialism rendered the individual irrelevant as postmodernism made the self the only meaningful reference point. Ultimately, this affirmed a series of trappings, tangible and shapeless, that proclaimed an identity of the self, a far cry from the national identity of the production ethos. Adorning the self became a goal, but not only with jewelry and clothing. An intangible dimension gained great significance.

Tourism, in which people acquire intangibles—experience, cachet, proximity to celebrity—became the successor to industrial capitalism, the endpoint in a process that transcended consumption and made living a function of accouterments. It created a culture, languid and bittersweet, and as writer Mark Edmundson put it "very, very self-contained. . . . There's little fire, little passion to be found," which had as its object participation in consumption. Yet even the young recognized that this culture was equally post-tangible, not about consuming things but about possessing experience. Material goods no longer fulfilled and created status in the United States and Europe. Only a very few products were so elite that they could not be widely owned and even those few could be suitably copied. Goods were not sufficient; status became a function of time spent, of context, of address, of place, of table in a restaurant . . . of experience. In the postindustrial, postmodern world, people collect the difference embodied in travel experience as some once collected Fabergé eggs. The act of travel, especially on terms dictated by the self, has come to mark the self-proclaimed well-rounded and allowed individuals to define themselves as unique. Travel as defining experience has become a new form of religion, a harbinger of a new way in which to believe and especially value the self. Bumper stickers will soon sport sayings like "she who has been the most places and stayed in luxury in all of them wins" instead of the more passé "he who dies with the most toys wins."

It is here that the wrapper of ecotourism becomes most clear. Although it is easy for people with education, cultural tastes, and social standing to perceive their activities as better than those of the widest swath of American society, the people who love Disneyland, to continue the fiction that such choices connote moral superiority is to belie the transformations of the last forty years. Even the hardiest mountain climber is the beneficiary of technologies developed in the space program that made every activity easier. People from Whistler Mountain have been known to say that the ski resort there was only possible because of Gore-Tex. Even if you live lightly on the land in your trip to Belize, the human waste that you leave is part of an ongoing threat to the coral reef most likely to draw you there. Even if you hike the Brooks Range in Alaska, shooting your food as you go—which is illegal by the way—your trip there came in some kind of internal combustion vehicle, you use modern equipment that both lightens your load and makes your experience easier, and your trip is still an interlude, an adventure with a beginning and an end that is a respite from daily life. As do the forms of tourism that are easy to regard as more base, ecotourism does what postmodern people need most: it tells them that they are special, they are important, that their activities and their lives are meaningful. This is the wrapper of the twenty-first century.

September 1998
The Outdoor Network

39

Cash Keeps Las Vegas Lush . . .

and It Should

THE DAY AFTER A RAIN, Las Vegas is one of the earth's most beautiful places. Moisture changes the look of the city, replaces the eternal layer of grime with a sheen of wetness. The blowing dust is down, and you can see forever. The great hotels of the Las Vegas Strip look like abstract expressionist sculpture in a landscape painting; could Christo have been here overnight? They glint against the backdrop of the mountains, stone cold and unreal with the snow-covered peak of Mount Charleston behind them. The angles are powerful, even sensual, the sense of time vast in the barren rocky expanses. The low scrub reflects light off the dark slopes. The colors of the desert, from the brilliant blue sky to the crumbly gray and golden richness of old mountains and the deep reds and purples of the surrounding rocks, come out with a vengeance. The scene is overpowering. It'll steal your breath, make you gasp in a way Americans usually reserve for the Grand Canyon.

But it doesn't rain very often in the desert. Las Vegas averages about four inches a year, and many years total rainfall is negligible. Most of the time, the dust is up, the valley enveloped in haze. The air is thick and crusty, the fate of all developed desert environments. The sun is hot, sometimes too hot even for the most devoted desert rat. This Las Vegas can take your breath away too, but from the exertion of even casual walking. Breathing is like inhaling in a blast furnace; it sears your lungs, fills you with flaming air, and, if you're not careful to hydrate, drains your energy. In the summer, people live before 10:00 a.m. and after 8:00 p.m. If you can help it, you don't go out during the heat of the day. It is so hot it'll make you wish for winter.

The desert Southwest is home to many of the nation's fastest-growing cities, and for the past fifteen years, Las Vegas has grown faster than any other metropolitan area in the United States. Since 1980, the population has grown from 480,000 to 1.4 million. In the 1990s alone, the population grew by 468,000, almost a 45 percent increase in one decade, spurred by an unbelievable building spree that added more than fifty thousand hotel rooms alone. Las Vegas's alchemy of entertainment, high wages for low-skill labor, huge construction projects, twenty thousand housing starts a year, and waves of retirees accounts for much of this phenomenal growth, but the ability to conquer the limits of the physical environment—hot and dry—lies behind it. Technological innovation, such as air-conditioning, became the catalyst for habitability. Without technological mitigators, only a desert tortoise could live on this edge of humid-climate culture. With them, Americans could do what they do best: put their faith in what the biologist Garrett Hardin used to call "technological solutions to all classes of problems" and impress the template of their society on any landscape they found.

Water for Desert Cities or Agriculture?

Have I mentioned water? It's the first thing anyone asks about growth in Las Vegas, Phoenix, Albuquerque, Tucson, and other arid western boomtowns: where will the water come from? The question is an obvious one, but asking it belies a fundamental misunderstanding of the way water works in American deserts. The Southwest uses more water per person per day than any other region of the country. In 1995, the U.S. Geological Survey reported that the per capita use per day in its Lower Colorado River district topped 121 gallons while the northeast used only seventy. And Las Vegas has endured countless water shortages since the 1940s, but never from a lack of supply. A lack of distribution capability, of pipelines and storage tanks, to keep up with spiking demand caused most shortages.

Nowhere does the American desire to use technology to obviate natural limits scream as loudly as the urban Southwest. The faith in technology that compels American society forward translates into sheer belief in the desert, and barring a revolution in the way American society does business, nowhere is there less chance of running out of water.

Water will always be the straw man in Las Vegas, the question the rest of the world asks that pulls attention from the real issues the city—and any booming metropolis in the desert—faces. In the American West, water is an institutional question instead of one of supply. Availability is not the question. Free-flowing water has become simply a question of fee per acre-foot, the standard measurement, of who will pay what for the water and who elsewhere will give it up. The only genuinely determining factor in acquiring water is cost. Even though water is the basis of life, it is still a commodity, marketed in the same way as any other consumable, and cash rules. This is the principle on which the American West was built. Author Marc Reisner astutely observed that in the West, water flows uphill to money. No place has more money than Las Vegas.

Despite the observations of such writers as Jacques Leslie—the old war correspondent-cum-water analyst who saw the hourly water show at the Bellagio on the Strip, where a display of water spans a thousand feet and jets shoot it as much as 240 feet in the air, choreographed to opera, jazz, and classical music, and observed that water in Las Vegas "is displayed more lasciviously than sex"—the distribution of water use in the Las Vegas Valley is surprisingly mundane. In the summer of 2000, Leslie's orgy of displayed water consumption—at the Bellagio and other resorts—accounted for 7 percent of the total used, according to the Southern Nevada Water Authority. Residential use comprised fully two-thirds of Las Vegas's water use, the nebulous category of irrigation claimed 9 percent, and all other uses—schools and government, commercial, and industrial—added 20 percent. The profligate display does what Las Vegas does best: it masks reality and on closer inspection confounds and deceives those who look only at the surface and actually believe it.

To be sure, Las Vegas uses water in a seemingly profligate manner: nearly four hundred gallons per day per person in greater Las Vegas compared to only 310 in Phoenix, the nation's next most profligate city. Yet the waterfalls, pools, showers, toilets, lawns, and golf courses of all of urban Nevada use only 20 percent of the state's water. The rest, as in every other western state, goes to agriculture and ranching, anachronistic activities that in Nevada only hope to survive when subsidized by the federal government. Eighty percent of the water produces a minuscule percentage of jobs, revenue, taxes, and other income for the state. Its gross handle of $1 billion per annum is less than 7 percent of the gaming win alone, and it looks even smaller when the gross income from tourism and entertainment are figured in. (And the numbers aren't that different elsewhere in the West. Even California, with its large agricultural economy, is similar. There, 80 percent of the state's water went to farming and ranching in 1990, while agriculture generated 2 percent of the state's gross income.) Nevada would miss the MGM Grand Hotel if it couldn't get enough water, but if all of Nevada's agriculture and ranching dried up and blew away, urban Nevada might not notice for years.

Water's for Fightin'

Reallocation, the latest bugaboo of the rural West, the process that figuratively takes water from the cotton fields outside of Yuma, Arizona, to water parks like the Schlitterbahn in New Braunfels, Texas, makes sense in Nevada and the region's other urbanized states. It's also a long-standing source of conflict.

Las Vegas's water story opens with the 1922 creation of the Colorado River Compact, the "Law of the River," the adjudication of the Colorado River that stemmed from California's growth and its imperial need for regional water. Los Angeles needed more water, and the Golden State's power let it take the river. Arizona fought, but little

Nevada just took its lumps, garnering all of three hundred thousand acre-feet per annum from the river, compared to California's 4.4 million. The relationship between California and its neighbors, the junior partners in western growth, was made clear: Like it or not, California would do its own thing. Nevada and Arizona could come along or resist if they chose. Their decision would not affect the outcome of water distribution.

So it remained until after 1945, when growth in the rest of the West accelerated as California blossomed into the twelfth largest economy in the world. Until 1945, most states didn't use their entire allotment. The Colorado Compact allocated more than 15 million acre-feet per annum to the various states, but the Colorado River routinely generated only 12 to 13 million in an average year. Someday, somebody somewhere was going to be left dry. California wasn't going to be the loser, and everyone else fought for just a little more. Nevada mostly stood by and watched, having long ago decided that when the big dogs tear into each other, the best survival strategy for the little dogs is to stay out of the way and hope nobody looks at you and licks their lips.

As the cold war ended in the 1980s and California's vaunted aerospace industry fell apart, the road to Las Vegas got crowded. Nevada grew, almost entirely in Clark County. Las Vegas, which had never needed its full share of the Colorado River, began to use first 60 percent, then 70 percent, and finally 227,000 of the 300,000 acre-feet allotted to it from Lake Mead. The numbers were a little misleading. Las Vegas, like nearly every other city along the river, received credit for the treated sewage it deposited in the lake, meaning that a lot more than 227,000 acre-feet came to Las Vegas in the average year. Still, reality aside, the die had been cast. Everybody's growth meant greater demand for water. As the twenty-first century dawned, the old western adage, "whiskey's for drinkin' and water's for fightin'," became even truer than a century before.

The battle commenced. The question became whether agriculture and ranching could hold the rural West's century-old share of the water at the expense of the cities, where upward of 90 percent of the regional population resided. Urbanization should have demolished the power base that rural interests long held, but that had yet to translate into reallocation. Urban growth came at the expense of rural areas. All of it shifted a greater percentage of population to urban centers and took western states farther from their rural roots. Every bit of that growth demanded services and above all water.

Las Vegas's upsurge in population quickly became a tidal wave, forcing a reassessment of its water situation. For most of its history, Las Vegas had been fed by the underground springs that gave the valley its name; in Spanish, "*las vegas*" means "the meadows," and the water that percolated to the surface there had attracted human beings since time immemorial. The railroad harnessed it, creating a private water company that distributed water to most of the city through the 1930s; a lot of people dug wells for their water too. As late as 1940, water seemed plentiful in the Las Vegas Valley, but the growth that started with the war and continued unbroken soon demanded new structures. Voters approved a municipal water district in 1948 to bring water from Lake Mead; and on September 22, 1955, Las Vegas received the first water in its new pipeline from the lake. It soon became insufficient to meet demand, and a new round of water infrastructure development began. In 1982, the Southern Nevada Water Project completed a pipeline that let Las Vegas take its full legal share of Lake Mead water. The artesian wells that long sustained the valley still pumped, but before their waters reached the surface, they were diverted to pipes that wound their way to all parts of the city.

The catalyst for both the shortages and the huge steps in infrastructure was one and the same: growth. Even before its remarkable 1980s and 1990s boom, the city had grown at a rate that consistently outpaced even the hope that infrastructure of all kinds could keep up. That happened even before 1985, when suddenly the rate accelerated to about a net gain of more than five thousand people per month or seventy thousand each year. All of a sudden, Las Vegas had much greater growth to contend with and the same flimsy infrastructure and weak traditions of leadership.

Political Savvy and Plentiful Cash Open the Taps

Into that vacuum stepped Patricia Mulroy, a visionary government leader of the sort rarely seen in Nevada or anywhere else in the West. As general manager of the Las Vegas Valley Water District, Mulroy intuited the future a good decade ahead of the rest of the West. In the 1980s, she looked around and saw that the nation had stopped building new dams. More water would have to come from redistribution of existing sources rather than the creation of new water projects. Mulroy recognized that reallocation guaranteed that the people who could use changes in the existing structure to their advantage would come home the big winners. But reallocation was a hard sell, an alteration of the status quo sure to enrage its beneficiaries. Circumventing them required a certain genius.

The innovation required a declaration of war, but as it turned out, only as a feint. In 1989, Mulroy and the Las Vegas Valley Water District fired an inflammatory salvo designed to do more than simply get the attention of rural Nevada. Mulroy claimed 805,000 acre-feet of water in twenty-six valleys across the state, some as far as 250 miles from Las Vegas. She claimed the Virgin River, an annual stream that starts near Zion National Park and winds its way to Lake Mead. Because it is not navigable in the nineteenth-century sense of the word, it had never been included in the water counted for the Colorado River Compact. This was more than a declaration of war. Despite Mulroy's promise that she didn't want to "wipe out" rural Nevada, the cow counties saw the water grab as social genocide. It was fightin' time in the new West.

It turned out not to be a fight at all, but the prospect of one brought other, more powerful, more recalcitrant, and newly vulnerable beneficiaries of the Colorado River to the table. A western water fight served nobody's purpose except the folks who didn't have enough water. Worse, it could shed light on the absurd and archaic arrangements that made fortunes for some and left others dry. The Colorado River Compact had become a fraud, an entirely outdated document that stemmed from a time when agriculture and ranching reigned supreme in most of the West and the cities were neither big enough nor sufficiently independent of the rural economy to grapple with farmers and ranchers. But the compact created a water oligarchy and as long as no one looked too closely and small-town universally Republican congressional representatives bartered their votes in statehouses and Congress, the rural West kept its federally subsidized prize. A great big stink about water in Nevada would do much more damage to the status quo than finding a way to give a little bit of water to cities to preserve the rural areas' larger prerogative of subsidized water for no apparent economic purpose.

Mulroy had something to offer them too. She could see a solution to the entire lower-basin mess that would only cost a few hundred thousand acre-feet of water each year. First she consolidated her power by bringing most of her opponents over to her side. Instead of building a dam and piping water to Las Vegas, Mulroy wanted to let the Virgin River flow. Rather than dam the river and create a huge fight not only with rural Nevada, but with environmentalists as well, Mulroy proposed letting the river go where it has since Hoover Dam was built: into Lake Mead. From there, two pipelines would take it to the Las Vegas Valley. Environmentalists were thrilled because Mulroy did not want to build a dam. Communities along the Virgin River were equally excited. Not only did they get water from the deal, but they also received seats on the newly reconfigured Southern Nevada Water Authority board, the new regional power in water. Pulling all of this off required major rethinking up and down the Colorado River, Mulroy reminded the public, but it was a start.

The grease for this wheel was cash, the real gold Las Vegas had to offer. Water has never been a paying proposition in the West. For a long time, the fundamental lack of economic logic simply didn't matter. Farmers and ranchers controlled the statehouses in the interior

West and that power, along with their well-placed representatives in Washington, D.C., guaranteed that no one seriously tried to cut the federal appropriations that covered the economic shortfall from the water that fed agriculture and ranching. The "law of the river" was really just oligarchic control by a well-placed and wealthy few defending privileges they'd never earned. That changed first when the cities of the interior western states grew and overwhelmed the rural areas and again when the Microchip Revolution altered the social meaning of American crops and natural resources. Did we really need that cotton from Yuma, Arizona? Did we really need to subsidize competition with farmers in the East, Midwest, and South with federal projects that couldn't meet their bills in the West? The fiction became harder and harder to sustain, and when Mulroy knocked, even people who probably hated her recognized that she brought a few more years of coverage for them by providing a solution that quieted the issue down.

Buying and Banking the Future

Mulroy's endeavors took care of Las Vegas's short-term needs. The long-term future has more to do with the larger trend in the West, the reallocation of water from rural to urban uses. In California, where reallocation was well underway as 1999 ended, water transfers occur within that huge state. For southern Nevada, reallocation of the river itself, as Mulroy suggested, was crucial. Again, Las Vegas's cash greased the wheels of water commerce. Irrigation districts have rarely been able to pay their bills in the West, and a shot of outside money is almost always welcome, if not a necessity. The cash came thanks to the creation of a water-banking system that let both Nevada and California "store" excess irrigation water in underground aquifers in Arizona. The irrigation districts were paid for putting their water underground, instead of spreading it aboveground to grow crops.

With computer models showing that even without an increase in the state's Colorado River allocation, southern Nevada could thrive with a system of water banking and leasing, Las Vegas had the rationale and the means to assure water well into the twenty-first century. The estimates suggest that Arizona farmers could provide the difference that Las Vegas needs to sustain its growth.

Full-scale interstate transfers of water have yet to occur, but they're not hard to see ten or twenty years down the road. They'll probably occur when a city like Phoenix has to curtail its growth because of an impending shortage of water. Then likely the water-rich upper-basin states, Utah or Colorado, will sell some water downriver. Although it is easy to imagine that rural interests would prefer to sell water anywhere but Las Vegas, most observers envision a system of water auctions, where money will talk. When money talks, Las Vegas will always be in the picture.

No U.S. city has ever ceased to grow because of a lack of water, and it's unlikely that Las Vegas will be the first. Los Angeles, Phoenix, Tucson, and the rest all found sources for their expansion and at least for now, Las Vegas has used its greatest asset, cash, to redirect enough of the water for long enough to buy the time to fashion a longer-term solution. As long as water is a commodity—and there is nothing in American society happening to change that—and Las Vegas has cash, the exchange will continue in some form or another.

March 2002
Urban Ecology

40

Stepping on the Air Hose

ON NEW YEAR'S EVE, the normally placid Gene pumping station of the Municipal Water District of Southern California at Lake Havasu felt like a military camp. Armed guards stood ready, people seeking bird-watching information were turned away, and the normally smiling faces were grim and drawn. It recalled those old black-and-white pictures from when Owens Valley farmers blew up the original California Aqueduct and forced William Mulholland's men to guard their treasured plunder. But this time, the tension felt different. A threat from Al Qaeda? More likely, fear of blowback from the collapse of the new Colorado River plan.

When the Imperial Valley Irrigation District voted down the transfer of water to San Diego County in December, it stepped on the air hose of an important cog in California's economy, the sixth largest in the world. Even the last-ditch attempt on December 31 to rectify the situation could not repair the damage. Everyone can now see that the Colorado River Compact, the Law of the River—what I've long described as the "fiction of the river"—is obsolete. A decade-long process of recrafting the agreement into a win-win situation for everyone seemed poised to succeed . . . until the district exercised its wholly owned selfish prerogative and threw public policy creativity into chaos.

All parties agree that reallocation of Colorado River water must occur. The Colorado River Compact dates from the legendary 1922 U.S. Supreme Court case, *Wyoming v. California*, when the court ruled the "first in time, first in right" presumption of priority in western water use applied across state lines as well as within states. Tossed aside by the court, upper river states like Wyoming and Colorado tried to reserve water for their own future growth—which they then imagined as agriculture—by letting California take most of the water south of Lee's Ferry, Arizona. They salvaged an equal amount for the states on the upper river.

That deal had all kinds of consequences but the most important was the creation of an agricultural oligarchy of federally subsidized water that persists until today. Water is power in the West and it is badly distributed. Three irrigation districts in California, including the Imperial Valley, hold priority rights to 3.85 million of the state's 4.4 million-allotment from the Colorado River. That leaves 600,000 acre-feet for the entire L.A. Basin and its more than 20 million people. In every western state, 80 percent of the water goes to agriculture and ranching. In no state, even California, do those activities generate 5 percent of the state economy. In short, every hour of every day, water goes to western agriculture because it always has, not because the crops it produces are necessary or it creates plentiful jobs or taxes on its profits fill state coffers. Subsidized agriculture also creates competition for farmers and ranchers elsewhere in the country who are not so fortunate to receive federal subsidies. Do we really need cotton from Yuma, Arizona, or alfalfa from the Walker River in northern Nevada?

Secretary of the Interior Gale Norton is the rivermaster, and she can hold states to the terms of the compact. By her decision, excess river water will no longer flow to California and Nevada. As a result, California will have to replace almost 1 million acre-feet of water this year if no accommodation is reached. Nevada will lose thirty thousand acre-feet. This is necessary, but it seems punitive and misplaced. Because of one rural vote, the cities that produce California's great wealth will feel pain and the agriculturalists who caused it will continue to drown their fields with impunity.

As direct as the secretary's action is, stopping the excess flow isn't enough. Secretary Norton should scrap the Colorado River Compact and reallocate water to reflect the realities of the New West. We are an urban society that produces its wealth in cities. Even though the water that irrigates that cotton outside Yuma now figuratively powers the Schlitterbahn, a New Braunfels, Texas, waterpark, reallocation screams for a bold federal role.

A new compact could take into account urban use, environmental legislation, new economic activity, fluctuation in water quantity, water quality, and countless other contingencies that didn't exist eighty years ago. It could create a Colorado River for the needs of today and tomorrow, not one beholden to a flawed past. Such a step requires the leadership to exercise federal power, anathema to the Bush administration.

Such a decision is about the economic recovery of the world's sixth largest economy. Even as greater Los Angeles rebounds, carrying the Bay Area and nearby states with it, the threat of a water shortage that hurts everyone looms over its head. The consequences of another fiasco could devastate a national economic recovery. Even more, the West deserves a better distribution of its most precious resource. Step up, Secretary Norton, shake off that antifederal cloak your administration wears, and swing away.

January 2004
Los Angeles Times

41

Las Vegas Deserves Some Credit

LET'S BE REAL. Despite your recent story on Nevada, the world of water has changed of late and the Southern Nevada Water Authority (SNWA) gets a good portion of the credit (*High Country News*, 9/19/05: Squeezing water from a stone).

SNWA reinvented water in the Southwest, changing a nastily competitive situation from the "whiskey's for drinkin', water's for fightin'" of legend to a cooperative model in which everyone has a seat at the table and people negotiate like grown-ups instead of like squabbling children. As a result, since 2003, southern Nevada has decreased its water use by fifty-two thousand acre-feet (one-sixth of Nevada's share of the Colorado River). At the same time, it has added about one hundred and fifty thousand people. No other American community can match that conservation record.

And regardless of the hullabaloo over groundwater in the Great Basin, in the Southwest, groundwater is a side issue, a hedge against future hard times. The real issue is the "Law of the River," the 1927 Colorado River Compact. Since its enshrinement, the compact has favored agriculture and ranching over urban use. As a result, 3.8 million of the 4.4 million acre-feet that California receives ends up in three rural agricultural districts. In a state where urban economic activity exceeds that of even the enormous agricultural industry by exponential factors, such an arrangement makes no sense.

We should devise a new Colorado River Compact, one that no longer inhibits job growth in urban areas. A new compact could begin by assigning the federally legislated water allocations on the basis of existing law. Prior commitments and legislatively mandated uses would come first. Then the rest of the water could be divided up among stake-holders, with preference going to the most economically efficient uses.

The funds this water generates would be divided among those who gave it up. In that way, two social goods would occur: the people who gave up the water would be fairly and justly compensated, and the water could create good jobs and prosperity for people who until now have been left out of the American dream.

Nobody should be forced to give up their water. Nor should anybody be able to stymie economic progress for their own selfish purposes. There is a happy medium, and we can achieve it.

November 28, 2005
High Country News

42

Power Play for a Stream

IT IS NOT OFTEN IN SOUTHERN NEVADA that we get to witness an attempt at a genuinely revolutionary act, but this past week, we saw one: Moapa Valley rancher Bob Lewis brought earth-moving equipment onto public land and illegally diverted a Lincoln County stream.

Lewis's actions were reminiscent of those of the fictional Joe Mondragon, the main character in John Nichols's *The Milagro Beanfield War*, a novel that turns on precisely the theme that Lewis seeks to exploit. In the book and the subsequent Robert Redford movie, Mondragon kicks over a sluice gate and illegally waters his bean field.

This small action, one simple kick, overturns the existing structure, and sets off a commotion that leads from the development community all the way to the governor's office. It is a riotous thumb in the eye of authority.

Of course, Lewis is hardly Joe Mondragon, and despite the tumult, he is unlikely to have his way. Instead of being revolutionary, Lewis is reactionary, seeking to turn the clock back to a time when ranchers with their federal subsidies ruled Nevada, when the first person who got his hands on any water got to keep it, no matter whether he did something productive with it or simply spilled it in the desert.

In that world, Nevada's power was in the rural counties. Nevada cities were small and weak, centers to which rural people came to trade, but largely irrelevant to the economy and the politics of the state. Boy, have things changed!

Lewis is making a "culture-and-custom" argument. He is saying by his actions that because he claims he once used that water, he is entitled to it forever. First in time, first in right, and damn the consequences to everybody else. That's the western way.

We're so far past that stage now that such an action is simply retrograde and backward-looking, a kind of self-indulgence we more typically associate with southern California. In the past fifteen years the world of water has changed dramatically.

For the most part, the battles about water have ended. In southern Nevada, we no longer fight about water. We negotiate. The premium is on cooperation, on bringing stakeholders to the table and letting them sort out the distribution of this precious resource.

Conservation is on the rise in urban areas—albeit with occasional setbacks—and the economic value of water used in urban areas so far exceeds that of rural use that it's hard to find any other explanation than culture and custom for the water that agriculture and ranching uses in Nevada.

And don't make arguments to me about the importance of agriculture and ranching to the food supply. Everything Nevada grows is surplus, pure and simple.

America will not starve without Nevada's alfalfa, a crop that consumes incredible amounts of water even by agricultural standards. And if you ate a hamburger three times a day, 365 days a year, the chances of taking a bite out of a cow that grazed in Nevada remain infinitesimally small.

The idea that rural and urban interests can sit down and negotiate water has been thoroughly underplayed. For those who write about water, it's been too easy to focus on conflict. It's a better story.

As much as I admire people who take a stand, no matter how cockeyed, this is a world of grown-ups now. Negotiation and compromise are the watchwords. Boring? Sure. In all of our best interests? Absolutely.

Nobody should be forced to give up their water. Nor should anybody be able to stymie economic progress for their own purposes. There is a happy medium and we can achieve it. We must sit at the table and negotiate with a clear understanding of every stakeholder's needs and wants. As the region grows, this question will become more acute.

Bob Lewis and his ilk make good press, but they don't get us any closer to solutions. In America, when you pull out the figurative hand grenades, you're showing that you do not have power. This is a sophomoric approach, little different from the late Edward Abbey pulling up road stakes in his precious wilderness.

Showmanship is grand, but if you're not at the table, you can't hold your own.

December 11, 2005
Las Vegas Sun

43

Solutions to

Water Overallocation

THE WORLD OF WATER has changed of late and it is about time. For almost twenty years, a gradual shift has been ongoing: water that was historically used for agriculture and ranching is increasingly going to western cities. Called reallocation, this process has become common throughout the West. It is so pervasive that the real question is no longer whether water will be transferred from rural to urban use. The debate concerns the terms of the transfer, how rural communities that cede water will derive fair and valuable benefits from it.

Although this process first gained momentum in California, the Southern Nevada Water Authority gets a good portion of the credit for its systematic implementation. Out of necessity, SNWA reinvented water in the Southwest. Nevada had received such short shrift from the original Colorado River Compact that the Silver State found itself backed against a formidable wall when growth in southern Nevada began to outstrip groundwater supplies. Forced to rely on federal dollars to ferry its trickle of the Colorado from Lake Mead to Las Vegas, southern Nevada faced a crisis in the 1980s.

The solution was remarkable: change from local water districts that competed with one another like baby pigs fighting for a sow's nipples to a regionwide model that put everybody on the same side and let them sort out their problems among themselves. Rivals became partners, changing a nastily competitive situation, the famed "whiskey's for drinkin', water's for fightin'" of legend, into a cooperative model in which everyone has a seat at the table and people negotiated like grown-ups rather than squabbling children.

In Nevada, this shared solution has already put an end to the travesties of yore, when communities opened up fire hydrants and spilled water into desert streets to maintain their claim to their "share." This century-old pattern of wastefulness had been common practice, the legal requisite for maintaining a place at the table. That situation bred bad behavior. Better planning and an original way of thinking about the distribution of resources has already led to significantly better outcomes.

Stunningly, Las Vegas has produced substantive changes. The city that everyone loves to deride has developed a powerfully effective water conservation program. Since 2003, the community has added more than a hundred and fifty thousand people. In 2005, the valley used 15 billion gallons of water less than it did in 2003, roughly 52,000 acre-feet. While such an accomplishment is always subject to backsliding, Las Vegas has saved one-sixth of Nevada's annual share of the Colorado River while adding a midsized city to its population. No southwestern city can match that accomplishment.

Such farsighted thinking is happening all over the region. The Salt River Project (SRP) in Phoenix has been a leader. Twenty years ago, 80 percent of the project's water went to agriculture and ranching. In 2003, SRP's water use was more than 65 percent urban. Phoenix's economy has carried the state, and SRP's leadership is a crucial part of Arizona's success.

In February 2006, the river states agreed to reshape the way the river is managed, with all seven states signing on. This step, which is based around drought management, has created administrative rules that put all the river states on the same side of the table. This is unprecedented, an extremely valuable step forward. But it alone is not enough.

Let's scrap the existing Colorado River Compact and write a new one for the twenty-first century. A new law of the river could take into account environmental legislation, the shift of population and income to cities, fluctuation in water quantity, water quality, and countless other contingencies that didn't exist eighty years ago. It could create a Colorado River for the needs of today and tomorrow, not one beholden to a flawed and long gone past.

A real "Law of the River" could begin by taking the federally legislated allocations of water and assigning those on the basis of existing law. Prior commitments and legislatively mandated uses would come first. This would allow for the fulfillment of federal mandates, make allowances for environmental and other kinds of legislation, and guarantee water for wildlife refuges, Native American communities, and others who depend on the river for survival. After these mandatory allocations, the rest of the water could be divided by participating stakeholders, who would decide the economic viability of proposed uses according to locally determined standards set in a regional, statewide, and ultimately interstate framework.

Once this water was divided, it would begin to generate income. The funds from it could be split between those who gave it up and the entities that administered the process. In that way, two social goods would occur: the people who gave up the water will be fairly and justly compensated and be able to go forward with their lives. We would also have the resources to maintain existing infrastructure and to expand it to meet new demand, allowing economic growth to continue.

Nobody should be forced to give up their water. Nor should anybody be able to stymie economic progress for their own selfish purposes. There is a happy medium and we can achieve it. We must sit at the table and negotiate with a clear understanding of every stakeholder's needs and wants. As the region grows, this question will become more acute. Attacking the real issue now rather than later puts us ahead of the game.

The solution is simultaneously revolutionary and painful: a fundamental reallocation of the river's resources must take place. We are an urban society that produces its wealth in cities and enjoys its leisure in open spaces. The water that once irrigated cotton outside Yuma now figuratively powers the Schlitterbahn, an attraction at a New Braunfels, Texas, waterpark.

These changes will not take all the water in the rural West. In fact, what I propose will probably take less water from farmers and ranchers than the existing process. Former Secretary of the Interior James Watt once remarked that he believed that administrative changes were more permanent than statutory ones. If he's correct, then the rural West is in greater danger now than it would be if a new Colorado River Compact was implemented.

In any reallocation, there will be winners and losers and those who give up their water must be treated fairly and compensated in a uniquely generous manner. The long-delayed agreement between California's Imperial Valley and San Diego can serve as a model. The deal could not be completed until the residents of the valley received safeguards for their economic future.

By centralizing water in an economically inefficient way, the existing Colorado River Compact impoverishes the future. It slows job growth in urban areas, making it harder for the middle class of the future to thrive. It even hurts democracy, for it makes it harder for people to find their way to a vested interest in the system. That water could create good jobs that lead to new mortgages, to prosperity for people until now left out of the American dream.

The economic realities of the twenty-first century scream for a new Colorado River Compact. American demography has long ago shifted south and west; national politics are inherently a Sunbelt strategy; the last American president elected without claiming Sunbelt origins was John F. Kennedy. Even in its worst moments, California is the world's fifth largest economy.

The result might very well be a kind of economic expansion we have not yet seen as well as better safeguards for nature, plants, and animals that we currently have. Not only can we erase nearly a century of bad policy, we can create a more efficient, fairer, more environmentally sound, and more productive system that lets more people have a shot at middle-class life. This revolution is already underway. We're really discussing its terms. The West deserves a better distribution of its most precious resource.

February 12, 2006
Newwest.org

44

Norton's Resignation Runs Deeper

than Norton Herself

THE DEPARTURE OF SECRETARY OF THE INTERIOR Gale Norton is hardly a victory for environmentalists. Who can blame her for fleeing a sinking ship? And after six years, nearing the middle of the second term? As the Bush administration has turned into the gang that couldn't govern straight, wise cabinet officials cannot be faulted for seeking a soft landing. Norton's timing is typical of departing officials even in popular administrations, and for her, the opportunities should abound. Little in her tenure made life difficult for anyone who might be inclined to retain her services after she leaves government.

But environmentalists should not cheer too long or loud. Norton was no prize, but there have been plenty worse. Her administration was clumsy and even inept; the recent effort to emasculate the long-standing most popular of federal agencies, the National Park Service, revealed the shortcomings of her management objectives. Ideologically, the message from Interior was consistent throughout her tenure; application of those ideas proved more difficult. Quite simply, the public objected.

While Norton's tenure at Interior has been widely and rightly perceived as disastrous for the environment, the secretary was never more than the instrument of larger forces. In her willingness to insert government into the marketplace to assist private business, in particular the energy industry, she followed the Bush administration's party line to a T. In her parallel unwillingness to use the tools of government to solve regional problems, she took a page from nineteenth-century secretaries who treated the office as a sinecure.

Norton's embrace of the energy industry was to be expected. Her roots in Colorado suggested a pro-energy development stance and she followed others of similar political persuasion to the office of the secretary. With a Wyoming energy man in the second seat in Washington—and don't forget, at the beginning of Bush II, many assumed he was the puppeteer—the revival of an energy development policy for the West was likely. The scope of what Norton and her contemporaries sought to implement was greater than many imagined, but arguably, circumstance outweighed intent in the emphasis on energy. The change in the nature of national dialogue that followed 9/11 allowed Norton to extend the boundaries of energy development with very little resistance.

Energy development dominated her years in Washington. The Arctic National Wildlife Refuge in Alaska (ANWRA) battle was the most obvious dimension of the effort to promote energy development, but it was a baffling choice of hills to die on, a largely symbolic waste of the administration's goodwill and energy. ANWRA was only a sideshow in a larger and more intricate process. If the goal had been pure energy development, a different strategy might very well have yielded greater results.

The secretary was not without guile. Many of the changes Norton implemented were administrative, effectively circumventing the publicity associated with legislative change. This has been the model for Republican secretaries of the interior since James Watt. During the 1980s, Watt attempted a wholesale revolution by secretarial fiat. Although it blew up in his face, the idea had enough traction to be implemented with considerable success nearly two decades later.

Norton's unwillingness to use the secretary's power as an instrument of resolution was equally consistent with her Republican predecessors. The signal operational strategy of her administration was hands-off. Effectively, the Department of the Interior turned its decision-making power over to the states and in some cases to counties within states. While turning back the clock to a 1950s-style states rights model has its admirable side, most of the problems in the West transcend state boundaries. In ordinary circumstances, this abdication of responsibility made little difference. In regional situations, leadership from Washington was sorely missed.

Sometimes, good results followed the lack of leadership, no thanks to this secretary. The recent agreement between the Colorado River states and last year's intrastate transfer of water in California stand as testimony. In both instances, the results stemmed from local and regional need and the creativity and willingness to negotiate of state-level officials. While an argument can be made that it was Norton's policy of hands-off that required state and local officials to be more creative, I'd have to dismiss that as sophistry. More leadership from the federal level, maybe even a little use of the enormous cudgel that the secretary of the interior can wield, and the process might have been easier and faster. And it could have generated more goodwill as well as greater cachet for future endeavors.

But you only judge people on what they do, not on what you think they should do. Although Norton pronounced herself satisfied with her accomplishments, I think she's being a little generous in her assessment. After almost six years, it's hard to find specific accomplishments to which to point. But maybe that's how the secretary wanted it. Still, if the goal was long-term change in the direction of policy, I don't think Gale Norton will be able to claim success.

In the end, Secretary Norton used the power of her office to turn the clock back in the West, to push the region back toward its history as a producer of the various fuels that drove American industrial power. She favored the sparsely populated rural West over its dense urban areas, and catered to the elements in Western society that emphasized the faux individualism of our region over the institutional arrangements that make the West function. Not the worst secretary of the interior by any stretch, Norton was strangely ineffectual in the role. Her departure is neither a triumph for environmentalists nor a loss for energy development. Much of the time, it'll be hard to know she's gone. And my guess is that few on either side will miss her very much.

March 14, 2006
Newwest.org

45

Keep Your Mitts Out of Our Kitty

SOUTHERN NEVADANS have so many reasons to dislike departing Secretary of the Interior Gale Norton that I cannot imagine that she would want to give us another, but she has.

On her way out the door from the gang that couldn't govern straight, Norton renewed her call to take 70 percent of the money generated from land auctions under the Southern Nevada Public Land Management Act (SNPLMA) and use it to defray the national debt. You have done too well, she whines, and you don't deserve the $2 billion we've raised from the sale of lands around you.

Wait a minute! A cabinet official in the most profligate administration in American history has the audacity to tell us what to do with the proceeds from SNPLMA? That takes a lot of nerve! The government that spent the American economy into oblivion now proposes frugality at the expense of Clark County. Stuff it, Madame Secretary.

The SNPLMA was drawn up for specific purposes. The law was to mitigate the impact of the development that would occur on the lands auctioned. It created a developable footprint in southern Nevada, allowing us to avoid a number of thorny environmental issues, and it divides the proceeds in specific ways—5 percent to the state's general education fund, 10 percent to the Southern Nevada Water Authority, and the remainder for quality-of-life and environmental purposes in the Las Vegas Valley and at Lake Tahoe.

It also put an end to the ongoing fraud that had occurred with what are called in-lieu exchanges, circumstances in which lands that the federal government desires in other places are traded for developable land in the Las Vegas Valley. Without pointing fingers, let's just say before the SNPLMA, the process stunk.

The SNPLMA has been a windfall for southern Nevada, no doubt. The run-up in land value that has accompanied the auctions has generated infinitely more money than anyone expected. With some of that land going for as much as $700,000 an acre, there is a lot more to mitigate the impact of growth in the valley.

At the same time, there is a lot more to mitigate. Growth and the rising cost of land has created a host of social problems, not the least of which is the almost complete absence of affordable and attainable housing in greater Las Vegas. With the average household income at around $50,000 and the mean home price in the vicinity of $300,000, it is safe to say that the average Las Vegas family cannot afford the average home.

Even more, it doesn't take a genius to see that the strain on our infrastructure is growing. Even as we build roads and schools, parks, and the whole array of other things our rapidly growing community needs, we are forced to rely on our own devices for a great deal of the work.

If you look carefully when you cross Interstate 15 headed west on the Las Vegas Beltway, you'll see the blue federal interstate sign give way to the Clark County beltway signs, desert tone in color. At that point, local dollars paid for that road, a remarkable achievement. No other community in America has undertaken such a task and accomplished it.

But that road serves people who live on land a good part of which became available for development under the SNPLMA. Local and regional government pays for countless other services that are necessary because of the development of that land. That's why we need the money and why we sought the law in the first place.

So, Congress made a law and Nevada got the better of it. After aboveground atomic and nuclear testing and the fiasco of the Yucca Mountain project foisted upon us by something called the "Screw Nevada" bill, isn't it about time we caught a break?

Where I come from, a deal is a deal. You make it, you live with it. In Nevada's sordid twentieth-century history with the federal government, we finally won one. No doubt. There's $2 billion in the kitty and it's ours. If you want it, Secretary Norton, come try to take it away. We will hold you and your free-spending friends accountable.

The SNPLMA should be the litmus test for Nevada politicians, the third rail of our dialogue. Anyone who wants to take even a dime of this money away from Clark County should be tarred and feathered and returned to the Bush administration, postage due.

April 2, 2006
Las Vegas Sun

46

Dumping Nuclear Waste

IT IS BACK! Just when you thought it was safe to go back into the desert, Yucca Mountain rears its convoluted, ugly head. Even after we've driven a spike in the vampire's heart, the darn thing refuses to die. A few signs of life remain, at least if you're a member of the Bush administration.

This time, the efforts to revive it reek of desperation.

This past week Energy Secretary Samuel Bodman spearheaded an administration effort to clear away obstacles to opening the dump— whoops, I mean the repository.

Basically, the bill sent to Congress this past week seeks to overturn Nevada law and diminish the regulatory structure that governs the site. No longer are they trying to persuade us that Yucca Mountain is scientifically sound, morally defensible, and nationally significant. The pretense is gone. With the same deft skill that took us to Iraq, they are trying to ram it down our throat. Science? Law? Out the window.

Former Governor Bob List can make an argument that we should accept the dump, but if he does it around me, he had better bring his good stuff. I will whack the lame tripe you have been spewing right back at you, Governor!

Yucca Mountain was a bad idea to begin with and it has gotten worse. The siting process has never been about science. It has always been about politics, and vicious power politics at that.

We were singled out for this one in 1987. Senator Bennett Johnston of Louisiana crafted legislation that insiders know as the "Screw Nevada" bill. Instead of two repositories, one east of the Mississippi River and one in the West, there was only to be one: Yucca Mountain. No more Deaf Smith County, Texas, or Hanford, Washington, the other two proposed sites, each with baggage equal to the Nevada Test Site. Only Yucca Mountain remained.

Where was science in this, then or now? Nowhere to be seen. The subsequent twenty years of maneuvering have been all about politics. No one seems to care whether the location can actually safely hold the nuclear waste. That is apparent as the administration seeks to increase the carrying capacity of the dump from 77,000 tons to 132,000 tons before they even have approval to open the darned thing. What's an extra 55,000 tons of nuclear waste between friends?

I hate to break it to the nuclear industry, but Yucca Mountain is beyond repair, crashed on the rocks of Nevada's newfound national significance. The phenomenal growth of Las Vegas and the ever-increasing role Nevada plays in national politics have combined to make Yucca Mountain a tenuous proposition.

Senator Harry Reid is the most powerful politician in this state's history, far surpassing Sen. Pat McCarran, the only other possible claimant. Reid gets a great deal of the credit for stymieing Yucca Mountain. The resolute objections of the rest of the congressional delegation have also helped. And Nevada's incredible generosity to both political parties has made it easier to get our point of view across. We have turned the tide on this one.

But we are not through yet.

The Energy Department has a long history of initiating projects with minimal attention to rules and law, and when faced with objection, arguing that since it has already spent so much money, it should just continue. After all, why not throw good money after bad?

This has become the rationale for Yucca Mountain. Instead of saying it is the right place to safely store the dangerous remnants that nuclear power generates, they now say "we promised the nuclear industry and we already spent a lot of money." This is perfect reasoning if your goal is expedience and you don't care a whit about the nearly 2 million people who live in Clark County, not to mention the 40 million who visit here annually.

We have held out against this scourge for a long time and have finally turned the corner. Each year since President Bush recommended Yucca Mountain for the storage of nuclear waste, the opening of the dump has become less likely. Even though List would like you to think the dump is inevitable, it is not. If it were inevitable, the nuclear industry would not be paying a fat fee for his services as its frontman.

April 9, 2006
Las Vegas Sun

47

Screwing with the American Vacation

THE CURRENT ATTEMPT by the Bush administration to cut the National Park Service operating budget by 20 percent is only the latest in a shameless series of efforts to gut the most beloved institution in American society. An administration that has taken pride in ignoring popular opinion now offers a gratuitous slashing that cuts at something Americans regard as a birthright. If you really want to piss off the public, mess with their vacations. "So what if the public's experience is affected?" these beltway divas are telling each other. "They won't be voting for us again."

Only six months ago, political hacks in the Department of the Interior tried to use administrative rules to shred nearly century-old protections of the nation's most cherished places. The public objected and they failed; now they are back, seeking to use a different kind of power to unravel some of the few remaining common bonds in our society.

I suspect that this too will backfire. National parks are one of the very few things Americans consistently point to as a visible symbol of their national identity. In their almost century and one-half of existence, the parks have been a crucial dimension of the glue that has bound Americans together as a nation.

Even more, the National Park Service, the agency charged with managing national park areas since its establishment in 1916, has consistently been rated the most loved federal agency by the American public. The keepers of the nation's sacred landscapes and treasured historic places connect with a public that is starved for meaning in a shallow age.

Even in a changing America, national parks retain tremendous psychic power. Created to forge a vision of what was special about the American nation—and not incidentally, to illustrate the differences between American nature and European culture—they remain icons that bind us together. Especially when you stand amid the parade of tour buses at Mather Point at the Grand Canyon, watching the Japanese disembark en masse, or join the constant stream of people to Old Faithful, you know who you are.

That has been the gift of the national parks. It is not the nature and the history preserved within that defines us, although that nature is often stunning and the history moving. The idea of the national parks is even more important than what they contain.

Especially in the West, national parks have become cornerstones of state and regional economies. From Montana to New Mexico, California to Colorado, every state counts on the jobs national park visitation creates and the dollars it brings in. I would hate to try to balance my state budget in the interior West without that revenue.

Economic arguments aside, if there is a greater American contribution to the application of the principles of democracy, I cannot imagine it. Before the eighteenth century, when people like you and I first got the individual rights we now take for granted, the idea of a public park didn't exist.

In Europe, everything belonged to somebody. Robert of Locksley, who we know as Robin Hood, happened along and saw the sheriff of Nottingham and his men arresting a man who killed a deer to feed his family inside the king's private reserve. The king's lands and animals were private, hunted only if the monarch allowed. All of it belonged to the liege. Robert objected, stove in the head of one of the minions, and found himself an outlaw.

Not here. National parks define the difference between the United States, full of land and promise, and hidebound Europe, where centuries of privilege weighed heavy on the backs of all but the nobility. Never mind that for a long time, our democracy was more symbol than reality. Until after World War II, only affluent Americans could easily visit their own parks.

Since then, the democratization of travel has made the national park experience available to the vast majority of Americans. Although minorities and immigrants are still underrepresented among park visitors, the park system received more than 388 million visits last year. That's a lot of people.

So this summer, when you visit the national parks, be sure to let your congressional representatives know what you thought about the reduction in service that this administration arbitrarily caused. I'm sure they will want to hear from you, especially with elections this fall. If the institution of the national park is important, the public needs to come to its rescue.

April 25, 2006
Newwest.org

48

Why We Need National Parks

I LOVE THE NATIONAL PARKS, both for what they are and what they represent about this country, but I have great fear about their future. I am afraid that both the public and park advocates take the parks for granted, in very different ways, but that unintentionally creates long-term dangers for the national park system.

National parks are a highlight of American democracy, one of our few genuine additions to the principle of a social contract between the governed and the governors. Despite the American conceit that we invented the idea of democracy, we didn't; all we did was tweak it a bit. National parks were one of the best wrinkles we put into the game plan of the Age of the Enlightenment.

Imagine what the idea of a "nation's park" meant in a world where all the land belonged to someone richer than you. Even if you never visited one, the very existence of such a place promised that the world could get better, that you, immigrant or native, urban or rural, could belong in this world, could find a way to be part of something larger.

I am deeply afraid that in twenty years, this will no longer be so. And when that happens, the votes in Congress necessary to provide the national parks with the funds they need may not be there either.

The public that loves the parks is still overwhelmingly white and middle class, precisely the segment that is diminishing as a percentage of the American whole. This group, while still tremendously numerous and influential, is very less likely to be so in twenty-five years. Given demographic trends, this constituency is likely to be a plurality instead of a clear majority before too long.

What will happen when senators and representatives whose states and regions depend on the parks have to negotiate with powerful blocs that have no appreciation for the institution? Will parks far away have the same appeal to the representatives of the future as they do to those of today?

National parks used to mean a ticket to Americanism, an experience at the very core of the meaning of national identity. Remember when it seemed like everyone had an "I Visited Carlsbad Caverns" bumper sticker on their car? It signified more than a vacation. Even today, people of a certain vintage get all misty-eyed when I bring up this long-forgotten symbol from their youth. More than anything, the bumper sticker made you part of something larger than yourself.

Today, that sense of belonging comes from commercial culture, from television and the airwaves, from music and *People* magazine. Where do Super Bowl MVPs want to go? Yellowstone? No, it's Disney World.

The point was driven home to me a few years ago, on a trip to Disneyland in Anaheim. There, I watched multitudes of Americans, new immigrant and native born, seeking and finding their identity in the embrace of Mickey and Minnie; this was defining, a way of being baptized into the state religion of our day, self-indulgent liberal consumerism.

This change in perception does not bode well, but even worse is the lack of communication between the conservation community and the larger public, the newest America. The immigrants of today represent the future of the country; so do the seemingly anarchic mountain bikers and the extreme sports enthusiasts of today. In twenty-five years, they will be stockbrokers and physicians, political brokers and voters.

I'm not certain they love the national parks like you and I do. And it is our fault. We haven't done a good enough job of competing with pop culture for the attention of the many. We haven't successfully explained what the parks mean, concentrating too much on their spectacular scenery. And more than anything, we have not connected with the new America, the urban, immigrant, Spanish- and Tagalog-speaking people, not to mention those who speak so many other languages so prevalent in cities in the West.

We are the most successful polyglot nation on earth; we are not perfect by any stretch of the imagination, but I will take our racial and ethnic problems over those of any European nation. In the United States, the potential to become American is always there. In Germany or France, that is simply not true.

But what does being American mean, especially twenty years from now? I would hope that appreciation for the beauty and meaning of national parks remains in 2026. If it does, if Congress in twenty years still thinks national parks are important, it will be because we have changed trajectory from the present. This is still possible. It requires more from all of us who love the national parks.

May 8, 2006
Newwest.org

49

Coping with Wildfires

FIRE SEASON AGAIN APPROACHES, and as always, we're prepared physically to fight the annual cycle of fires that sweeps the western United States every summer. The fire bosses have congregated, the computer models and the weather reports are ready, the training has begun, the Hot Shot crews are poised, and the smokejumpers stand prepared for the call. Bring it on!

Psychically it's a different story. Americans no longer know how to deal with wildfire.

We used to suppress it. With the settlement of the West more than a hundred years ago, fire became the enemy and the remedy became suppression—putting out every fire as soon as possible after it started.

The policy began when the U.S. military fought fires in nineteenth-century national parks, carried on into the Forest Service, and became standard operating procedure for all federal agencies.

The pinnacle of suppression was the 1930s 10:00 a.m. policy. Under it, all fires were to be put out by 10:00 a.m. the morning following the first report of fire. This leap of faith required a strong belief in the human ability to control nature that wasn't always born out in experience, but it made for a clear and strong objective.

Stopping the fires before they started was equally important and it took a different guise. "Remember, only you can prevent forest fires," Smokey the Bear told generations of American kids and adults, and the charming bear persuaded us to put out campfires and crush out cigarettes. This too had its shortcomings, but it gave the public something to aspire to.

For seventy years, this was the mode of fighting fire in the West, and it worked—more or less. Oh sure, there were a couple of big blow-ups—the mythic 1910 fire season, when most of the northern tier burnt, is the most well-known—and these made headlines throughout the nation. But by and large, firefighters fought fire off well enough and the policy of suppression persisted in the 1960s.

Then came one of those sea changes, a new way of looking at the world that transformed fire management. In the 1960s, fire scientists and ecologists realized that suppression had a serious downside. When every fire was put out, it meant that the amount of fuel—plants, dead timber, and the like—available to burn increased dramatically. Fire, it turned out, served a natural function. It kept vegetation down and made fires burn less hot and consequently less destructive. Forests that burned on an annual and every-few-years cycle turned into meadows; when fire was suppressed they again became forests. A little bit of fire, it turned out, did a lot of good things.

So we tried something new: controlled burning, a name for the practice of allowing fire to burn for the purpose of making later fires less severe. This idea went under many names and had many dimensions, but the overall goal was the same. Use natural fire—lightning and the like—or introduced fire, fires started intentionally in accordance with the plans of specific federal agencies, to lessen the damage from catastrophic fire and sometimes to recreate historic environments. This too worked well, within reason, but it was truly playing with fire. And when people play with fire, whether in Greek mythology or in modern America, they sometimes get burned.

The burning began in the most dramatic of ways, with the torching of Yellowstone National Park in 1988. It has continued off and on, culminating in the disastrous Cerro Grande Fire at Bandelier National Monument in New Mexico in 2000 that nearly destroyed Los Alamos, the town where the atomic bomb was developed. Rodeo-Chideski, Hayman, Biscuit, and others followed in a hurry. When controlled fire escaped or natural fire was allowed to burn, they sometimes created exactly what the policy was supposed to prevent: catastrophic fire. Not only did these fires destroy hundreds of thousands of acres, they also sent the entire idea of controlled burning up in smoke.

It leaves us with a dilemma, one that seems particularly poignant this year, as the West suffers through another year of drought and the fires inexorably begin. We can't just suppress, nor can we always control the fires we let burn.

The problem is not with the land managers; it is a problem on the land itself, one visible to anyone who hikes in any western forest. Suppression may have worked too well and thirty-five or so years of controlled burning have only treated a small amount of western land. It is a tinderbox out there, folks!

So we face a devil's bargain. Our responses are too small for the problem and the consequences of failure are too great to imagine. After thirty-five years of controlled burning, the Park Service, the most aggressive federal agency in implementing the practice, has managed to treat 2 million of its 80 million acres. The Forest Service, with much more land, is only now implementing plans to routinely use fire as a tool. We may have waited too long to fully implement introduced fire on western landscapes.

So now we are in a bind. If suppression isn't applied, communities that have encroached on the forests and ridges of the West—and there have been no shortage of them from the Colorado mountains to the California coast—can expect to find themselves very hot indeed. Political leaders echo the cries of their constituents. Put the fires out now; save lives and property. Smokey the Bear's still around too. Now, like everyone else, he's got his own Web site.

But controlled burning has become anathema to the public. We can't really let fires burn, even when they're natural in origin and far from people. We've been singed too many times in recent years and fire managers and the leadership in every federal and state land management agency are rightly a little nervous about letting fires go. The implications if one gets away are great; the ramifications are too big to risk.

But we can't just suppress either. All we do is defer catastrophic fire to a later date, fully aware that every day a fuel load builds is a hotter, more destructive, more difficult fire to contain. Politics and science have crossed swords and there are no easy answers.

So the crews are ready to fight the fires once again, and we all hope that the rains come early. A new model for western fire management has yet to emerge, but one must. We see the beginnings of a new flexibility in the management plans of individual forests and in the overall planning of the National Interagency Fire Center in Boise. Suppression will remain necessary, the default response when fire threatens lives and property. Controlled and natural burning will increase on public land as a way to avert the enormous fires we have seen in recent years. As a working strategy, this is sufficient; as a master plan, it is only a start.

June 23, 2006
Newwest.org

50

A Super Regional Water Authority

Now that the hearings about the Southern Nevada Water Authority's plan to build a pipeline from rural Nevada to Clark County have come to an end, we should pay attention to the inevitable jockeying for position that is sure to follow.

A process is under way beneath the radar of most of the public. For almost twenty years, a gradual shift has been ongoing: water that was historically used for agriculture and ranching is increasingly going to western cities.

Called reallocation, it has become common throughout the West and has already taken place in Nevada. Reallocation is so pervasive that the real question is no longer whether water will be transferred from rural to urban use. The debate concerns the terms of the transfer, how rural communities that cede water will derive fair and valuable benefits from it.

Although rural interests see the Southern Nevada Water Authority's effort as an unbridled water grab, their point of view is simultaneously hysterical and grounded in the reality of life in rural Nevada. I admire them for defending their historical interests, but I cannot agree with their point of view.

Rural Nevada has always detested the Silver State's cities even as the urban parts of the state pay the bills for the hinterlands. Clark County routinely generates almost 80 percent of the state's revenue, and that money is spread throughout the state like lubrication. If Las Vegas dried up, the rest of Nevada would be in a world of hurt in a hurry.

But acrimony is useless. Maybe there is a better way. What if we were to expand the concept of the Southern Nevada Water Authority, the idea that we are all in this together, beyond the county line? What if White Pine County could be brought into a newly created super regional water authority, governed by a set of binding principles? This might allow for better discourse as well as creating a situation that allows everyone to have a piece of their cake and to eat it, too.

Such a system might change this discussion. Under a new set of terms, a fairer system could result. A baseline could be established, with the use of water evaluated in legal, economic, social, and environmental terms. Prior commitments and legislatively mandated uses would come first. This would allow for the fulfillment of federal mandates, make allocations for environmental and other kinds of legislation, and guarantee water for wildlife refuges, Native American communities, and others.

After these mandatory allocations, the rest of the water could be divided by participating stakeholders, who would decide the economic viability of proposed uses according to locally determined standards set in a regional framework.

Once this water was divided, it would generate income. The proceeds could be split between those who gave it up and the entities that administered the process. In that way, two social goods would occur: The people who gave up the water will be fairly and justly compensated and be able to go forward with their lives. We would also have the resources to maintain existing infrastructure and to expand it to meet new demand, allowing economic growth to continue.

Nobody should be forced to give up their water.

The solution is simultaneously revolutionary and painful: A fundamental reallocation of resources must take place. We are an urban society that produces its wealth in cities and enjoys its leisure in open spaces. That fact will not change.

A super regional water authority will not take all the water from White Pine County. In fact, what I propose will probably take less water from farmers and ranchers over time than the existing process. Former Interior Secretary James Watt once remarked that he believed that administrative changes were more permanent than statutory ones. If he's correct, then rural Nevada is in greater danger now than it would be if a new arrangement that created seats at the table for every stakeholder governed Nevada's water.

October 8, 2006
Las Vegas Sun

Global Power for America. Photo by Virgil Hancock III.

Part IV
Looking Beyond Las Vegas's Borders

Introduction

Why This Nation Needs a Statue of Responsibility

WE HAVE NOW HAD 230 YEARS of this little experiment of ours called American democracy, and I am not altogether convinced that the Founding Fathers would entirely approve of what we have done with their ideas. It is a long way from there to here, but they would certainly be mystified at our vision of freedom.

When Paul Revere looked across at the Old North Church to see if the British were coming by land or sea, he had a pretty good idea of what freedom meant. In the world of the eighteenth century, freedom was the right to do as you pleased within the confines that your larger community established. This was more than enough in his era; after all, they were less than a century removed from the Salem witch trials.

But Revere and his revolutionary compatriots were onto something. Freedom in their world was not the province of the individual. It was a right granted by nature and the Deity, enforced by the judgment of all around. In essence, the community created a large psychic space, and individuals were free to careen around as long as they did not bust the boundary line.

Today, freedom is about the self. In our age, we see freedom as the right to do what you want, where you want, how you want, when you want, and with whomever you want. Like much else in our society, freedom is exclusively defined by the individual. It has little to do with larger concepts like community.

Now it is hard to complain about this change, given the rights revolution of the past sixty years, but it has cost us something important. In Paul Revere's day, people understood that rights came bundled with obligations. We have somehow left the latter part of this equation out of our calculus.

We have a Statue of Liberty to enshrine our rights. It sits in New York harbor, its torch thrust upward, a symbol of American freedom. It is a thing of beauty, a powerful image that defines us to ourselves as well as to much of the sane world.

What we are missing is a Statue of Responsibility, a reminder of the way rights and obligations are intertwined. I cannot imagine what this would look like, but I think I have the place for it: Alcatraz Island in San Francisco Bay. This former prison, the site of an occupation by Native Americans, would be perfect for a symbol of what we owe. It would be a bookend, one on each side of the country, giving us a vision of the transcontinental link between the two components of American freedom.

Imagine that! A society in which people gave their obligations to community and nation the gravity they now only feel for their personal rights. People would act differently; they would participate instead of whine, they would vote rather than sit on the couch changing channels, and they would challenge what the media and politicians put forward.

In that America, vibrant discussion would take place—as it does today—except that its governing principle would be the betterment of community, not the feathering of the individual nest. People would engage those who disagreed with them, rather than blow them off in the caustic and vituperative manner of too many of today's commentators. You know the type, people who would rather win than be right and will stop at nothing to have their way.

Of course, the discourse was no more enlightened in Paul Revere's day than it is today. In 1798, just twenty years after the signing of the Declaration of Independence, the Federalists, John Adams's party, passed something called the Alien and Sedition Acts. These nefarious laws outlawed criticism of the party in power in an attempt to save a failing administration from defeat at the polls.

So, nobody is perfect. Still, I'm entranced by the idea of a Statue of Responsibility, a counterpoint to the overemphasis on the individual that pervades early-twenty-first-century America. Done properly, such a piece of symbolic art could illustrate the many ways rights carry obligations with them.

Thomas Jefferson reminded us that "eternal vigilance is the price of liberty." In this day and age, we are sufficiently vigilant, but not always in the right ways.

July 2, 2006
Las Vegas Sun

51

Do We Really Need the Rural West?

DAN DAGGET, THE WELL-KNOWN AUTHORITY on western livestock grazing and a seemingly mild-mannered guy, lost his cool and fairly screamed at me: "Why don't all of you go back to the cities back East you came from and give us back our West!"

I didn't know what to say, and I'm not often speechless. I'm not from a city, and I'm sure as heck not from anybody's idea of back East. My sin was to ask the intellectuals holding yet another conference espousing the pastoral northern Rockies as a model for the rest of us in the West, "Why do we need the rural West?"

I always cringe when people from the rural West tell the rest of us how to live. There's an arrogance to their pronouncements, a foolhardy pretension that they are real and that the 95 percent of us who live in western cities somehow don't matter.

The truth is that they—not us—are the exception. Montana and Wyoming don't lead and, at this stage, don't have much to teach the rest of us. They're the ones without a real city. Oh sure, Cheyenne, Bozeman, and Missoula might claim city status, but by the standards of Phoenix, Las Vegas, Albuquerque, or even Boise and Santa Fe, they're just towns. They don't have the sprawling freeways or the concentrations of retired people the rest of us do. They don't have real airports. Plus, they're overwhelmingly white.

In Nevada, more than 1.5 million of the 1.8 million people in the state live in Washoe or Clark counties, home to Las Vegas, Carson City, and Reno. Phoenix and Tucson contain more than 3 million of the state's 4.5 million people, and that doesn't even include the corridor effect to Flagstaff and the autonomous Navajo reservation, one of the last places in the entire West with a large, diffuse, rural population.

The question the rural West can't answer is: why should the rest of us subsidize their condescending culture and custom arguments? The rural West sure doesn't pay the bills—look at tax revenues in any state and you'll see that clearly enough.

It uses nearly all the water and generates nowhere near the revenue from it that cities do with a lot less. And its industries, ranching, agriculture, timber, mining, and the like, are tossed on the scrap heap in our transfer payment, federal, tourist-based regional economy.

The truth is hard, but clear. The rural West has become a playground, a colony the rest of us visit when we want to relax or indulge our fantasies. We camp, hike, swim, boat, bike, ski, hunt, fish, and ATV throughout the rural West, making our living and our lives in its increasingly stretched out and stunningly dense cities. We may dream of a home on the range, but that dream is usually just a way to cope with the traffic on a freeway headed to or from the office.

The importance of the old rural West has ended and it's never coming back. The Microchip Revolution, which has made information transfer more important than the raw materials the West used to export and has turned experience and leisure into currency, is upon us. It's a little early to declare an end to the natural resources–based world economy, but at least in the United States, natural resource extraction is approaching anachronism.

Historically, this country's advantage was always cheap land and cheap labor. Since World War II, land hasn't been inexpensive, and while American labor remains the most valuable in the world, it's also far more expensive than in many other countries. In this new world, trees have more value as scenery than as timber, and a mountain will likely generate more revenue from the skiers who whiz down it than from any animal grazing its slopes.

There's a solution, and I'm only half kidding: go to the ranchers and farmers and tell them that we'll give them their best year plus annual cost of living raises to match inflation, and in return they'll give us their water.

They can pretend to ranch and farm; they can lay out center pivot irrigation systems that'll spin around and around, but no water will come out. They can pitchfork invisible hay from the back of pickups to invisible animals, and they won't even have to worry about inevitable fluctuation in crop and animal prices.

In the meantime, that roughly 80 percent of the water in every western state can go for job creation, jobs that pay taxes, that don't require federal subsidies, that have futures for the ever-growing number of young and immigrants who flood the region. They're the middle class of the future, the ones whose wages will fund the Social Security of today's middle-aged workers. The sooner we propel them upward, regionwide, the better off we'll all be.

We'll give up something, sure. But discarding a myth that has deceived us for a century may be the healthiest thing this region can do.

April 24, 2000
High Country News

52

Western Growth and Class Warfare

DON'T GET ME WRONG. I'm no more a fan of urban sprawl than the next guy. I bought a house on the outskirts of Las Vegas eight years ago, only to find that three years ago I was surrounded by town. We moved farther out to get away, but didn't see the handwriting on the wall or the bulldozers following us. Twenty thousand new housing starts a year gobble up a lot of space, and before we knew it, we were surrounded again!

Still I've grown really tired of the arguments people make against growth in the West. From Chelsea Cogdon and Jeff Gersh in their award-winning film, *Subdivide and Conquer* and James Howard Kunstler in *The Geography of Nowhere* to ranchers and federal and state land management officials who rail about the problem but contribute to it by their actions, there's something disingenuous about the antisprawl movement.

They say sprawl is bad because the world was once better, because people could see farther and had fewer neighbors, because they knew one another and shared in a community, governed by a set of rules that they all agreed upon. C'mon, folks! Could such an idyllic world exist if it was populated by human beings? The noise of the well-meaning that surrounds sprawl obscures the vista.

The people who have been in the West the longest and the people who are the most recent arrivals have formed a dangerous pact. The newcomers exemplify the tree house effect: they're the last ones in, trying to pull the ladder up behind them. The "stickers," as Wallace Stegner used to call them, have been here a long time—you know the kind of testimonial that begins: "I'm an eighth generation westerner and . . ." as if it conveys some kind of divine right—and now see dollar signs when land developers trudge up to the old family house. They complain about growth but throw in the towel as soon as a developer pulls out a checkbook.

I can't help but see these pleas for the status quo as nostalgia and yuppie-class entitlement masquerading as mythology—the longing for a West that never was. The solutions and strategies that captivate these people scare me. The ideas of regulation and green space—the Portland, Oregon, and Boulder, Colorado, models—sound grand, but they don't solve the problems and in fact may even make them worse.

In the 1960s, Boulder levied a sales tax to buy its own green-belt around the city. It's beautiful, it's wonderful, and a cyclist like me can pedal forever along its paths. But the green space has become a moat that made Boulder an exclusive island amid an ocean of Front Range growth.

Boulder's residents are the occupants of a baronial fiefdom. They live in the castle because they got there first. The rest of us have to cross the moat on the drawbridge of narrow highway to enter the sacred city and serve our self-proclaimed betters. Back to your suburban tract home, knave! Back along the crowded ribbon of concrete, made worse by Boulder's successful fight to prevent the widening of the road. This is their idea of a better community, democracy and justice, of fair play?

The growth ring around Portland, drawn in the 1970s, worked for a while, but it too had nasty side effects. The Rose City became a white city, defined as much by class as anything else—and a cynic might say consciously recognizing the link between race and class. Portland became a city where white people would live downtown, where the rising cost of property preserved older neighborhoods by making them too expensive for anyone who wasn't well-off. The limits to outward expansion let the middle class stay close by, eliminating what they feared. "It's a miracle," the New Urbanists like Kunstler say, a city with a downtown that functions after dark and public transportation that functions to boot. Diversity in today's Portland is teenage grunge.

The solution to growth isn't green space, a growth ring or even zoning. All these remedies achieve visible goals, but none solve the larger problem: how can we live in an increasingly diverse society and get along?

I know one thing for sure: allowing the rich to hide behind moats of green space is not the answer. That strategy reminds me of the castles the crusaders built in the Middle East almost a thousand years ago. All of them offer incredible views, for they sit well above the surrounding plain. But the crusaders weren't building up there for the view. They took the hilltops because they couldn't tame the valleys, couldn't come to grips with the world around them.

Within a couple of generations, most of the castles were empty, the crusaders dead or gone back to Europe. It is an instructive lesson about exclusiveness that the New Urbanists should take to heart.

July 6, 2000
High Country News

53

Las Vegas Since 9/11

THE ATROCITIES OF 9/11 clearly upset the calculus of the postindustrial world, and Las Vegas felt that intensity more than almost anywhere else. The shock was immediate and it hit hard. On September 14, when McCarran Airport reopened, the town emptied and cancellations galore began. Conventions, individuals, groups, overseas travelers all slowed initially to a trickle, and even if you wanted to come, it was hard to find a way. Visitation dropped, some said to half of pre-9/11 numbers. Suddenly, Las Vegas's lifeblood, the 36 million visitors a year who haul our sled, the ones who pay sales tax and leave money in the slots, on the gaming tables, and in restaurants, box offices, and shops, was threatened.

The attacks made tourism vulnerable, piercing the previously impenetrable armor of the new Las Vegas, America's first city of tourism, the leading city of the consumption of entertainment. Las Vegas is built on the ability to get people here cheaply and in a hurry. For the previous fifteen years, the formula worked almost perfectly. It has been go, go, go, through good and bad times elsewhere. We built almost seventy-five thousand hotel rooms, added new dimensions in entertainment, shopping, and even world-class restaurants. In the process, the city's image dramatically changed. We went from pariah to paradigm, from the weird edge of American society to a central place in a national culture increasingly devoted to entertainment. It all seemed to go up in smoke in an instant. The short-term impact was harsh and quick; layoffs at the major hotels for the first time in a generation were a small part of the new picture. Only Hawaii, overwhelmingly dependent on air travel, suffered more among American tourist destinations.

In fact, the attack may have had a greater impact on the state than on Las Vegas. Recent numbers show that not only is there a slight decrease in the state's revenue, but that an even greater problem exists. The 3.7 percent drop in gaming revenue is the worst on record, but the state's optimistic projections, predicting a gain of 5.9 percent, made a difficult situation even worse. The impact on the Strip is worst, reemphasizing the dependence of the state on Las Vegas. Local cynics may wink that the crisis exists because of the governor's habit of manufacturing crisis so he can ride in and save the day, but we're still the horse in a one-horse state.

That horse took a beating last September but by the first week in October, the visitation numbers were resurgent. The weekends were back to par; the weekdays were running at about 65 percent capacity, about 10 percent below normal. The airport announced that traffic had returned to 91 percent of normal. But a return of visitors was not the same as a return to normal. The hotels responded with a time-honored mechanism, offering deeply discounted rates to visitors. This, MGM Mirage spokesman Alan Feldman noted at the time, was a "double whammy," fewer people in rooms that sold for less. In a move that could be construed as panic, they extended those offers to the end of the calendar year and beyond, locking themselves into lower revenues and then, in some accounts, trying to alleviate their losses with layoffs. It was a tense fall and early winter in the most unionized city in the nation.

A year later, it seems that the impact of 9/11 on Las Vegas is likely to be a large but short blip on our longer-term radar screen. Since that horrid day, many have suggested that a new, more serious age has begun. We're more aware, more tuned to international issues, more concerned with the ideal of democracy and the meaning of freedom. In reality, it seems much more like a concentrated effort to turn the clock back to September 10 and get on with the business of being American. After more than half a year in a state resembling war, the nation is not significantly different. Jerry Springer is still on the air, the new season of

Sex in the City is under way. This isn't World War II, when we endured rationing and shortages, or even the paranoic state associated with the Korean Conflict. Instead, most of the time, for most Americans, this has been an offhand kind of war, one that only intermittently effects the population as a whole. An occasional upgrade of the threat alert or the odd claim of overhearing terrorists plotting on a cell phone have a direct impact, but people celebrate and mourn, live and die as they did before that fateful morning. Day-to-day life seems to go on as it always has.

At this most basic level, little has changed. We live in a society where experience is currency and entertainment has replaced culture, where people pay for their cable TV ahead of their water bill and turn off the air-conditioning to preserve their HBO. A wide swath of the American public regards leisure as a right and not as a luxury or even a privilege. They self-indulgently seek release at almost any pretense. Ultimately that's good for a Las Vegas that can continue to do as it has for the better part of half a century.

Yet 9/11 placed some new issues in high relief for us. First and foremost, in an unbelievably perverse way, it further erased the old stigma, the canard that Las Vegas was the capital of sin. We'd become smug in our importance as a center of leisure, seeing Las Vegas as a global symbol of the new culture of pleasure and even daring to link Las Vegas's success to the great run-up of the 1990s. We counted our overseas visitors with pride, pointing to the expansion of the reach of the city's magic, pushing into worlds of people now or soon able to experience Las Vegas's particular allure.

Instead that dark day showed the limits of Las Vegas as a symbol. Our reach remains the western and industrialized worlds. To the despicable Islamic extremists behind this atrocity, Las Vegas was no more nor no less decadent than any other place in the non-Muslim world. The institutions they chose for their vicious attack were economic and political. Leisure was not on the list, for what gain could be achieved by attacking Americans at play? Instead, these westernized killers used Las Vegas as does everyone else: as a place to play. The tawdry image of killers-to-be enjoying a veritable Last Supper here, morphed into Osama Bin Laden himself stuffing dollar bills in a stripper's G-string in the tabloids, suggests a confusing role for Las Vegas, as a place out of time, a meeting ground of instinct, but also a place apart from the wicked picture Al Qaeda drew for itself of American and Western society.

September 11 also taught us much about the economics of tourism. Las Vegas's prosperity is based in something tangible, people's ability and desire to travel. In the postindustrial world, tourism is the one industry that hasn't been subjected to the exporting of jobs; you still have to visit to receive the experience. And here we've brought them more and more by air. Since the expansion of McCarran airport in 1963, Las Vegas has been shifting its mode of visitor delivery from regional automobiles to national air travelers. In the early 1960s, the city remained a regional destination; as many as two-thirds of visitors came from California by car. With the opening of the C gates in 1988 and the D gates a decade later, those percentages were reversed. By 2000, nearly 70 percent arrived among the 36 million who annually passed through the airport.

The attacks upset travel so quickly and completely that almost instantly Las Vegas experienced its first downturn since the start of the Mirage Phase, the thirteen-year building spree that began with the opening of the Mirage on New Year's Eve, 1988–89. When I strolled through the airport one afternoon the week after the attack, it was nearly empty. The airport reported a 28 percent drop in passenger traffic for September; visitation for the month fell 14.1 percent over the previous year, the first such decline in memory. Airline companies curtailed their flights by as much as 20 percent, almost certainly guaranteeing a decline in annual visitation. If the seats weren't there, people couldn't arrive by air and with 70 percent of visitation arriving by air, the math was obvious.

Despite such powerful numbers, the impact was exaggerated and temporary. The real vulnerability of tourism exposed by 9/11 turned out to be air travel alone. That's why Hawaii suffered so much; it is hard to drive across the ocean and no one has the time to visit the islands by ship anymore. Las Vegas's numbers quickly sunk in September and October, but auto destinations like Reno showed little impact at all. Even more, the local market in the North shows continued albeit small growth. The impact of the attacks was specific, on air travel, rather than on travel in general. And Las Vegas's desirability as a destination quickly showed. After the initial slowdown, visitors returned . . . a growing percentage by car. While the days of the 1960s, when driving Californians dominated visitation are unlikely to return, the traffic on I-15 grew in some counts by 15 percent. The even more gargantuan traffic jams that will surely ensue threaten to do what the legalization of Indian casino games in California has not as of yet accomplished: it may finally make the traffic on I-15 the problem of casino magnates instead of individual drivers.

The attack also disrupted the generally harmonious labor-management formula that has been crucial in Las Vegas's growth. Since the completion of Hoover Dam, southern Nevada has always been short of labor. The Mirage Phase and all the jobs it created made that shortage even worse, and the Culinary Union revived its fortunes by filling the casinos' needs. Las Vegas became the "Last Detroit," the last place where you can be unskilled, make a middle-class wage, and have it mean something in America. Yet labor remains a huge fixed cost for casinos, and after 9/11, as many as ten thousand service workers, unionized and otherwise, were laid off. Animosity developed between the union and management, and when contract renewal came up in spring 2002, the situation was ripe for conflict, for the settling of scores that stemmed from the rocky post-9/11 months.

The quick and mostly bloodless resolution of the new contract illustrated another impact of the attacks. In the new climate, everyone was squeezed, union and hotels alike. The hotels were highly leveraged to begin with; the drop in stock prices before 9/11 increased their vulnerability. The only way to catch up was with lots of happy customers;

for that, the hotels needed their workers. A work stoppage was out of the question; who would pay the bills for even a weeklong strike? The Culinary Union, rebuilt since Las Vegas's last major strike in 1984, had seen the post-9/11 layoffs threaten its recent history of success. But the Culinary could afford a major strike no more than the hotels. Its coffers had been depleted by attempts to keep laid-off workers afloat, and its cohesiveness as an entity had been challenged as people had to choose between their group and their individual needs. Even in the tension in May and June, the end result was always clear. The hotels and the union were going to continue the partnership that had led to so much success for both. The big Strip companies settled first; they had the most to lose. The bigger downtown hotels followed soon after, leaving a few outliers. All but one came to the table and the eight-day strike at the Golden Gate, with its 175 workers out of 48,000-plus in the union, became a symbolic confrontation, not a truly meaningful one. The status quo has returned; it remains to be seen if the profits of the 1990s will again follow.

The casinos receive credit for avoiding the major ill plaguing American business these days, the criminal inflation of earnings that has led to the defrocking of a few of the business elite and widespread distrust of their peers. To their credit, the casino companies took their economic medicine—mostly before 9/11. The precipitous decline in stock prices that dogged the industry after falling earnings in 2000 and 2001 had turned upward before this spring's discouraging news. Even more, this historically suspect industry has to date weathered the biggest financial scandal to rock American business since the depression of 1929. As yet there's no evidence of funny stuff in casino industry accounting, making casinos and entertainment the one dimension of the new economy to survive the fall of the dot.coms. The boys, the old Mob guys, must be turning over in their graves. Their commercial descendants are the good guys as the economic leaders that once castigated them now experience well-deserved scrutiny and scorn.

Even more, the casino companies remain a solid investment for many. After watching the devaluation of Silicon Valley and the demise of "new economy" giants Enron and WorldCom, as we watch older blue chips like IBM and GE plummet, the relative value of casino stocks looks very good. Most of the majors are on the rebound, well up from their lows in 2000 and 2001, and the tight regulation of cash by federal and state law provide a bizarre insulation from the Wall Street shenanigans that continue to stun investors in other sectors. Recent numbers show upturns in profitability and casino prospects seem solid. They perform a service once regarded as ephemeral but that now seems critical: they fill the American desire for leisure. I've often said that I'd rather have my money in entertainment than in automobiles. Little in the current situation makes me want to rethink that proposition.

Nor has the aftermath of 9/11 slowed migration to Las Vegas. All tourist towns are at their core real estate markets, and Las Vegas's twenty-year population boom clearly illustrates how visitors become residents and bring new residents in tow. Our growth differs only in its breadth and diversity from that in other tourist towns; not only do we import the served classes, we house the folks who provide the service as well. The outrageous real estate costs of small mountain towns of the ski industry keep their workers well out of town; the beach is too expensive for all save professional athletes, movie stars, and Third World dictators. Only in Las Vegas can the "visited" live where they serve the visitors.

The stunning news that 9/11 slowed population growth not at all stems from the most transformative feature of the valley, its graying. Retirees become a more prominent part of the region every year, and in many ways, they are residents who behave much like visitors. Major consumers of entertainment, meals, golf, and even gaming, retirees have already reshaped the face of the valley. They constitute a newly diverse economy, a sector that will continue to grow almost no matter what, something borne out in the last ten months. In the next decade, retirement will continue to transform the region, spawning a different service economy with its logic.

Yet they are the point people for another of the dangerous social issues that our politicians avoid, the ludicrous mechanisms we have for paying for the state. Get it straight, folks: everyone who lives here and everyone who moves here takes more out of the system in services than they put in in dollars. We depend on growth to cover the ridiculous structure of the wobbly stool of state revenue. The money it generates saves us from taxation, but it brings people who share in the same benefits. Despite being in the top ten in income, we're near the bottom in state-provided services. While the editorial page of the *Review-Journal* might laud such a condition, it is slowly and steadily strangling the state. We're drowning in private prosperity and public services go begging. As the population ages, passing bond issues will get harder and harder. Lord knows it's already hard enough. Bond issues for fire and police go down to defeat; even library bond issues have failed! The quality of life is suffering and will get worse. The state simply can't be sustained under the current system. Tax revenue is too unstable and demographic change is quickly ruling out the referendum.

Visitors may never notice such local issues. Las Vegas's most brilliant alchemy of recent years has been its ability to blur the distinction between reality and unreality. Las Vegas has been reality with the rough edges planed smooth, a place better than real for so many visitors. In New York, New York or Paris Las Vegas, people clearly and consciously chose the unreal over the real, preferring the Las Vegas imitation for all kinds of reasons. The French aren't rude to you at Paris Las Vegas, no matter how they treat you in Gay Paree.

Yet in the aftermath of 9/11, reality and unreality did more than blur: they became indistinguishable. Expressing their grief, people came to New York, New York, itself built without the Twin Towers, bearing flowers and photos, creating a votive, a shrine to our national loss. It mattered not a whit that this was New York, New York and not the real New York. The hotel stood in for the real city, creating the context in which one dimension of the catharsis of our national pain could take place. People cried at New York, New York as if it were the real New York.

As strange as this sounds, it sums up the crimped nature of the impact of 9/11. Las Vegas seems to have largely experienced a short-term impact. Despite the shortfall in state revenues, the long-term picture is brightening. As the numbers come back, as migration continues, and especially as people ignore the differences between real and imitation, Las Vegas continues to provide Americans and international visitors with what they want. Our genius has always been to simultaneously reflect and anticipate desire, to see what people want now and to figure out what they'll want tomorrow before they do. September 11 upset some of the premises that underpin this strategy, but it now seems, not for long. Even in hard times, people demand leisure and Las Vegas exists to fill that niche. Increasing visitation is an encouraging sign, as is the recent rise in casino profits. It appears that the counterintuitive economic miracle of Las Vegas will continue. We will pay the lion's share of the state's revenues and routinely the legislature will short Las Vegas and Clark County. This happy-sad scenario is the best we can hope for unless the state's leaders get some real stones. Of course, whether that happens or not, another attack could well mean all bets are off.

September 2002
Las Vegas Mercury

54

Steamboat Springs's

Feisty Sense of Self

OF ALL THE PLACES TO SKI, Steamboat Springs, Colorado, is my favorite. It's the "town that skied," not a ski town, or a field or a ranch that became a resort, an invented ski town recreated by outsiders or started from scratch. In Steamboat, skiing didn't replace something else; it wasn't a stopgap for a fading economy, nor a way to rescue the town from doldrums. In Steamboat, people skied because they had to and because they loved to. Throughout the first half of the twentieth century, there was no better way to get around and nothing that made the process more fun. As it skied, Steamboat Springs became special: it was a town with a fixed sense of itself, an identity that possessed considerable cachet; it became a town of champions, of winners, of American standard-bearers as skiing swept the nation. Skiing produced Steamboat's personality long before it generated the dollars that became the basis of the local economy.

Three things set Steamboat Springs apart from its peers, giving it depth, strength, and power as well as the basis for friction. Steamboat retains a strong local identity based in its history. It has a powerful idea of what constitutes "home," a sense of community, and a long tradition of local activism and power. It has a history of other economic activities besides tourism that includes raising water-glass-sized strawberries at the turn of the twentieth century, ranching, mining, and agriculture. All of these things combine to create a powerful and committed community possessed of a strong self-identity, able to influence the direction of the community and its many assets in all kinds of ways.

At the same time, the very traits that bolster community can create friction, leading to the self-description of Steamboat Springs as "one feisty town."

Steamboat's history made it unique among communities that embraced skiing. Located far enough from the Front Range, it remained apart until the completion of the Moffat Tunnel in 1927. With peak snowfall topping 260 inches, sixteen feet of snow atop the mountains and as much as four feet consistently on the ground in an average year, the area was cold and remote before winter sports became widespread. In such a place, cars went up on blocks in the winter and so skiing was both birthright and obligation. All the children, boys and girls alike, were raised on skis. "I learned so early I have no recollection of it," Carol Rickus, who was born in 1918, recalled. All were proficient by the age of seven, and many depended on their skis for communication during the long winters. In one instance, Marjorie Perry, the iconoclastic daughter of a family with coal and railroad interests, made skiing into a obsession; she was renowned for skiing to Denver and back, a 320-mile round trip. These circumstances led to the creation of a strong local culture based in skiing that valued Steamboat Springs in a way that communities created to become resorts simply could not.

Steamboat Springs may be the only ski town in the West with community festivals that were begun by locals for locals. Winter Carnival, today a draw for tourists as well as locals, began in 1913, when Steamboat was routinely snowed in for the winter. The people who came to the early carnivals were locals in search of conviviality that the winter did not easily yield, not tourists looking for something to do. The event was for locals; like Daniel Boone and his turkey shoots, the carnival made a pageant from the skills necessary for survival in Routt County. Ski racing and all it embodied, individual prowess, competition, hardiness, and determination, was prominently featured, carved like a slalom turn into the core of Steamboat's personality.

This fierce identity helps set Steamboat Springs apart from other mountain communities. Steamboat has always been a small town, self-contained and different from not only the cities of the Front Range, but from conventional resorts. Steamboat always possessed a sense of its own permanence. As some small towns cherished their high school sports teams, the heroes of Steamboat Springs were its locally born and bred skiers. "We are first a town and then a resort," the community said in countless ways, and the town came first, sometimes even at the expense of profit. Steamboat has a stronger sense of home than any of its peers, simultaneously making it easy to define and hard to reconcile with changing trends. It is not an accident that Steamboat was the first and most successful of the mountain towns to embrace the concept of subsidized affordable housing, nor that it was responsible for stopping the construction of the resort at nearby Lake Catamount. People see Steamboat as "one feisty town" with good reason. The town can be at odds with itself and with the ski companies that run the mountain.

Steamboat's identity is based in part on the accomplishments of its many championship skiers. Carl Howelsen, the great early-twentieth-century ski jumper for whom Howelsen Hill is named, was first, and he put the town on the map. Steamboat produced champion skiers, including Gordon "Gordy" Wren, Werner, and Billy Kidd, all Olympians and among the most venerated skiers of the postwar generation, almost as an afterthought. Steamboat Springs possessed cachet; it was a town of winners, of American standard-bearers in the new sport sweeping the nation. For a while in the 1950s and 1960s, Western State University in Gunnison, nicknamed "Wasted State" by its afficionados, won the NCAA ski championship every year—with a fresh crop of skiers directly from Steamboat. The town went by the nickname "Ski Town USA," and one skier came to epitomize all that meant: Wallace J. "Buddy" Werner, for whom the mountain and the city library is named.

No American skier of the 1950s and early 1960s had quite Werner's persona. The five foot nine, 145-pound Werner was the first American to triumph in a major European downhill event, won countless other ski races and competitions, and was honored by nearly every skiing organization in the United States. Possessed of a breakneck style and a modest, easygoing demeanor that belied an aggressive competitiveness, Werner lost many races in spectacular falls. His kamikaze, hit-or-miss style endeared him to the skiing audience. Werner seemed somehow real, like them, human, ordinary, and typical. He did not understand the concept of surrender; even after he fell, he rose and skied maniacally and always awoke the next day ready to race again. "I never look back," he was known to say. "If I crash this week, what the hell? There's another race coming up next week. If I ski as hard as I can, maybe I'll win it."

Buddy Werner epitomized Steamboat's culture. Like everyone else, he skied. The sport was the legacy of a cold, snowy, high-elevation mountain town; racing was an afterthought for Werner, who quarterbacked the high school football team while doubling as first chair cornet in the high school band. Did he run out onto the field at halftime in uniform?

Werner was the best example of what makes Steamboat Springs special. In a town where people measured the severity of winter by the number of ten-inch strands of barbed wire covered on a fence by snowpack—the famed four-wire winter of local legend—life required zest, the willingness to push hard and grab fast at what came by. It required relying on your neighbors as much as it did refusing to relent. Coming from this culture, Buddy Werner's championship caliber racing was not a surprise. Werner was the ideal representative, the most proficient at an essential local skill that defined who the town's people were.

This combination of history, personality, and grounded reality gave Steamboat Springs the best set of tools of any ski town when it came to dealing with change. Steamboat mounted the most sustained and successful resistance to the transformation of the town by the development of resorts. Unlike Aspen, Vail, or Sun Valley, Steamboat Springs was home to generations, with strong, closely held ideas of appropriate values and responsible social behavior. It had mechanisms, ranging from political and civic institutions to public protest, that could be harnessed in support of local values, the elusive concept of home.

Even in the face of widespread development, Steamboat Springs reconstituted itself as a new place capable of defending its new definition of home. The town redefined itself, carving a new identity that nodded toward Buddy Werner's hometown, but blended disparate elements together as it shaped an ongoing role for the town as the resort became more important to the region's economy. Steamboat Springs was no longer Buddy Werner's hometown, but it was a place that could revere his spirit without stretching credulity. Werner's tradition lived on, reconstituted around the values of people who embraced what his town represented. Home could mean a lot of things, but most of all in tourist towns, it meant a place where locals, natives, and recent arrivals rated as highly as did visitors. In Steamboat Springs, this was an accurate description more often than in any other ski resort. Buddy Werner might not have recognized everything about the Steamboat Springs of the 1990s, but he would have understood the fierce way its people guarded what was most precious to them: their idea of home and the identity it gave them.

September 2003
Steamboat Springs Magazine

55

Put the DOE on Trial

A COUPLE OF YEARS AGO, I called for the indictment of the U.S. Department of Energy on charges of ongoing criminal conspiracy at Yucca Mountain under the terms of RICO, the Racketeer Influenced and Corrupt Organizations Act. The sneak visit to Las Vegas in 2001 of then–secretary of energy, the smug and oafish Spencer Abraham, prompted my almost tongue-in-cheek column on the subject. Abraham was expected to visit my kid's school during his brief trip. I contemplated a hopelessly sophomoric guerilla raid: me and a pair of dimestore handcuffs sans key would make a citizen's arrest and initiate RICO proceedings. When I told my wife of the plan, she asked me how I'd like being single again. I contented myself with the printed word.

It turns out I was right on the mark. Yucca Mountain was a bad idea to begin with, but worse, it is a fraud, a dishonest effort designed for the sole purpose of siting the dump—oops, excuse me, the *repository*—in Nevada, whether the Yucca Mountain location is appropriate or not. The Energy Department has long subsumed its stated goal of "sound science" to the political desires of dump supporters and then to the objectives of the sitting administration. The series of e-mails that exposed this criminal fraud only confirmed what we all knew: they add to the fundamental mistrust of the process and to the wide contempt in which the Energy Department is widely held in the Silver State.

Nevada has a nearly twenty-year history with subterfuge on this question. It began with the "Screw Nevada" bill, the 1987 legislation that made Yucca Mountain the only place the Energy Department studied for a waste repository, and continued for a generation of dishonesty that included the hiring of former Governor Robert List, who took big money to shill for the project in the 1990s, and a generation of attorneys who did their best to make the project seem a done deal. The administration of George W. Bush provided cover; the objections of every responsible elected official in the state seemed to mean nothing.

But now the truth is out. U.S. Representative Jon Porter is using his subcommittee to conduct hearings into the fraudulent e-mails, and the entire Nevada delegation has turned out to flog the culprits. U.S. Senators Harry Reid and John Ensign made the unusual gesture of attending the hearing in the other house, lending the imprimatur of the Senate to the proceedings.

At the very least, this will delay the process and give us a more public forum than the courtroom for our claims. With more of the stiff backbone we've seen of late and some perseverance, we'll win a battle against this flawed and corrupt process and the idea behind it.

May 5, 2005
Las Vegas Citylife.com

56

Learning from Santa Fe

THE TUMULT ABOUT COST OF LIVING in the Las Vegas Valley continues, with complaints about a lack of low-cost housing and the ongoing shortage of workers becoming more acute. No one here seems to have a plan, much less a solution. But other communities that grapple with similar problems have begun to pursue remedies.

In the West, Santa Fe, New Mexico, has gone farthest in that direction. For my money, Santa Fe is the most fraudulent tourist town in America. Its fabricated version of the historic past plays on the American love affair with individualism and the romance of national expansion and conquest.

On its famous plaza, with Indians selling jewelry on blankets under the facade of the old Palace of the Governors, Santa Fe smooths the rough edges off of the Spanish, Native, Mexican, and American experiences in the West, repackaging them as kitsch and art for a high-tone, free-spending crowd.

The differences between Las Vegas and Santa Fe are real. Las Vegas knows what it is. Santa Fe has pretensions. Even though Santa Fe represents history and culture to its visitors and we offer entertainment so malleable that we change what we are to meet every whim, Las Vegas is a lot more real than Santa Fe will ever be.

Still, tourist economies share all kinds of characteristics. A decade ago, Santa Fe's average annual income in tourist service jobs was $12,000 while the average house cost $220,000. That's simply not doable. Since then, housing costs have risen to a mean of $278,233 in 2005. As in Las Vegas, the service industry wage has not kept pace.

To solve this, Santa Fe has tried something unprecedented: the city has enacted its own minimum wage, $9.50 an hour in 2006 and $10.50 an hour in 2008. The decision ripped into the core of this little town, pitting the different versions of hipness that the community harbors against one another. It also puts the small mountain town in league with fourteen other states and the District of Columbia, all of which have enacted their own minimum wage that is higher than the federal base of $5.15 an hour.

Nevada voters joined this parade, passing our own version in 2004. If voters in 2006 again ratify the 2004 vote, the minimum wage in this state will rise to $6.15.

Turns out that even such action might be futile. The impact of higher wages at the bottom end of the scale has only a limited effect on the overall economy. Economists now believe that small increases in the minimum wage do not hinder economic growth. Only about 7 percent of the work force is affected and none of the fourteen states with a higher minimum wage lost jobs.

In all, lower-income people live better. One single mother, an assistant hotel housekeeper in Santa Fe named Manuela Soto, told the *New York Times Magazine* that the two-dollar-an-hour increase would allow her to pay bills faster, cover increasing gasoline prices, and purchase more school supplies for her sons.

It's hard not to see in Santa Fe's action a harbinger of the future of tourist communities in the West. Every such community faces this very problem. The cost of living has spiraled out of control so dramatically that, in most places, wages and housing prices have no relationship to one another. Santa Fe's remedy is likely the first such measure at the community level, not the last.

Thanks to the high level of unionization in our workplace and the consistent shortage of labor, our wage scale is high enough that trying to solve cost of living problems with an increase in the minimum wage at the local level makes little sense.

Like Santa Fe, our problem remains the difference between wages and the cost of home ownership. An increase in the minimum wage alone won't solve that.

But Santa Fe's new law should be a wake-up call. It is another stick in the eye, another warning that we can't continue like this. If working people cannot live decently on the wages they receive, something will give.

A higher minimum wage might not be the remedy for the Las Vegas Valley, but the 2004 vote suggests that such grassroots issues are in play in 2006. Whether they influence local and state politics remains unclear, but if Santa Fe's experience is typical, local leaders especially should expect grassroots pressure this year and in the future.

January 22, 2006
Las Vegas Sun

57

HOAs Are a Necessary Evil

EVERYBODY HATES HOMEOWNERS' ASSOCIATIONS. The renowned social critic Mike Davis calls them "microscopically parochial interests" and others describe them as a tool of developers wielded against the homeowners they're supposed to serve. Even my students groan at their mention.

In a society that prizes individual rights above all else, homeowners' associations are oppressive, parochial, tyrannical, and downright mean.

Everyone, or at least anyone who was late with an association dues check, has their horror story. They built a back porch that was not even visible from the street and spent a year wrangling with the self-important people on the architectural committee. A missed payment racked up thousands of dollars in fines.

Nobody, except developers and the tight-lipped creeps who run for board seats and want to snoop in your backyard, likes homeowners' associations. Nobody, not even members of the boards themselves, trusts them.

But homeowners' associations play a significant role in the new Las Vegas, one that makes those of us who are willing to put their civic rights in a blind trust, and stipulate to property values as the pinnacle of American civilization, tolerate them. Especially in transient places such as Las Vegas or where larger, communitywide institutions are in decline—which is to say everywhere—homeowners' associations stand for what remains of the social fabric of the mythic America.

With confidence in state and national government at an all-time low and local government increasingly regarded as the province of special interests, the homeowners' association is a hedge against decline. They have become the closest thing to the grassroots democracy Alexis de Tocqueville envisioned when he wrote about the United States in the 1830s. At the same time, they assure the conformity of image that is at the heart of stability in a liberal consumerist society.

All you have to do is look at neighborhoods without associations. Usually, they are less consistent, more erratic, and worn. Nice houses abut those with trashed yards, broken windows, and cars on blocks. One bad house on a block ruins all the homes around it.

Done properly, homeowners' associations function in place of community relationships, of the shame of being the worst house or yard on the block, of sharing life with your neighbors.

In more than one middle-class subdivision in Las Vegas, the homeowners' association fee pays for maintenance of front yards. Close enough to feel insecure about the potential of their streets to fall from desirable to the dreaded "transitional," neighborhoods embrace an ethic of enforced order. Every lawn is eternally and uniformly green and manicured.

But by default, homeowners' associations assume an undefined role that inspires resentment. In Las Vegas neighborhoods where houses turn over at astonishing rates, where proximity and sociability are often unrelated and most life goes on in walled-in backyards, the temptation to hire a semiprivate pseudopolice force to protect the value of your single largest investment is vast.

No wonder that even people who aren't crazy about such organizations accept them. Homeowners' associations maintain what passes for community. You can complain about your neighbor's dog without confronting your neighbor.

In a strange way, the homeowners' association smacks of an earlier America, one in which Paul Revere might be comfortable. Revere and his eighteenth-century contemporaries understood individual freedom as something located within the community's standards. They were free to do as they pleased, they thought, within the boundaries that the community established for behavior.

The reach to homeowners' associations as tacit reflections of community standards, albeit, a cynic might say, of a lazy and dissolute community, is not hard. The community stood in for the individual and the individual agreed to abide by the rules—as long as they primarily applied to other people.

But everyone still hates their homeowners' association and the rules it makes. They want to restrict others and not themselves, more evidence of a self-indulgent, self-centered world where people have abandoned any conception of mutually agreed-upon coercion.

The issue is larger than Las Vegas, but it has manifested itself in our new suburbs.

Almost every new home in Las Vegas's future will be part of a homeowners' association. A bland but oppressive authority at the grass roots follows, where board members inflict their personal biases on their neighbors to the echoes of resounding resentment. Tocqueville's democracy? Closer to the world of novelist Neal Stephenson's *The Diamond Age*, where authorities tattoo "poor impulse control" on the foreheads of miscreants. Twenty-first-century community has its own pitfalls.

March 12, 2006
Las Vegas Sun

58

Remembering the Chernobyl

Nuclear Disaster

TWENTY YEARS AGO THIS PAST WEEK the nuclear power plant in the Ukrainian town of Chernobyl erupted in a fireball that spewed radioactive particles across much of the Northern Hemisphere.

Thirty-one people died as a direct result of the explosion, twenty-eight from acute radiation poisoning or thermal burns. Another nineteen died soon afterward, and nine known fatalities from thyroid cancer are direct results of the accident.

In a ten-kilometer radius around the plant, coniferous trees and small mammals received lethal doses of radiation.

Twenty years later the consequences of that disaster are everywhere: in the destroyed communities around the plant, in the shattered lives, in a changed physical environment, and especially in the deformed children who abound throughout the immediate region and well beyond.

Only a craven government, insensitive to its people, would allow the conditions that led to this disaster. It could only happen in a place such as the Soviet Union, where people did not have rights. Not in my country, you say. Not here, in the USA, where the voice of the people is heard.

Don't kid yourself.

While we have had no disaster comparable to Chernobyl, the U.S. government has displayed an equal disregard for the health and safety of the American people. From Bikini Atoll to southern Nevada, from Alaska to New Mexico, Americans were put at risk when officials knew better.

After one test on Bikini Island in the late 1940s, U.S. servicemen were sent in to scrub the radiation off abandoned ships used in the test. An old rancher outside of Baker, southeast of Ely, once told me that the day after an aboveground test in the 1950s, his sheep were covered in white dust and showing signs of sickness.

Two men in what he described as "spacesuits" showed up on his doorstep and insisted that he sign a piece of paper—a release—in exchange for a $5,000 check. The old man shook his head; he didn't feel he had a choice.

Ask the downwinders in southern Utah, the people who experienced the consequences of aboveground testing. Terry Tempest Williams, the noted Utah writer, calls her family "the clan of the one-breasted women," because so many have had mastectomies. They lived under the fallout; the wind blew it right onto them.

Americans have a profound distrust of nuclear power. The 1979 movie *The China Syndrome*, in which a reporter discovers a cover-up of an accident at a nuclear power plant, may have been bad science, but it almost perfectly mirrored public discomfort with the nuclear industry.

The movie coincided with the scariest real event in this country, the Three Mile Island accident in Pennsylvania. We actually evacuated the area around the plant, the kind of thing you only see in science fiction movies. No doubt, nuclear technology seemed bigger than the people who managed it and maybe even eternally beyond their control.

With such a history, it's no wonder the last new nuclear power plant in this country opened in the 1970s.

Now we face energy Armageddon. We are an oil basket case, unable to heed warning signs such as $3-a-gallon gasoline while we drive SUVs and trucks that drain gas like a thirsty man guzzling water under the hot desert sun. There is the possibility of shortages in electricity generation in the immediate future.

We will face a critical choice, whether to change behavior or to find new sources. We can only tighten the turbines so much, only wring so much power out of existing mechanisms. With the growth in demand for electricity, we are going to have to find new sources.

The most obvious and probably the easiest answer will be nuclear power. It is already being pushed at us. The question remains whether the public will accept what it perceives as the risk of nuclear power.

The noted columnist George Will once told me he thought the future would chastise us for not embracing nuclear power. I told him I thought the problem was the callous and dismissive treatment of the public by government and industry. No wonder the public fears nuclear power—look at its experience.

I don't know whether nuclear power is safe. I do know that I have been given plenty of reasons not to believe the Energy Department and the nuclear power industry. If they want to get me to sign on, they are going to have to earn my trust. And telling me that we have to do it and blowing off my questions won't get them there.

April 30, 2006
Las Vegas Sun

59

Remembering Memorial Day

LIKE A LOT OF AMERICAN HOLIDAYS, Memorial Day used to have a great deal more meaning and considerably less partying associated with it.

In the small town where I grew up, Memorial Day was the time for old soldiers to put on their dress uniforms—if they could still fit in them and sometimes even when they could not—and parade through town on their way to the cemetery.

These World War II veterans had a special air about them; now firemen, clerks, and plant workers, they were transformed into the young men who won the war that made the world safe. In solemn tones, they publicly remembered the losses we, as a nation and as individuals, had borne.

Even at the height of the Vietnam War, the least popular with the public until the current Iraq fiasco, the ceremonies had meaning and powerful resonance. They brought generations together, reminding those who supported the war and those who opposed it of a shared loss, of a common bond of loyalty to their country.

Sacrifice, a word that has disappeared from our national lexicon except in the most callous of ways, loomed large in those days. It was part of a shared culture, communicated in an array of ways in almost every dimension of public discourse. It helped define national identity, making people feel like they were part of something bigger than themselves—however flawed it appeared at any given moment.

Now before you write me off as some misty-eyed nostalgic for a past that never was, remember that I make my living explaining how the country has changed. The new America, the one of instant communication, infinite choice, and gargantuan celebrity, has much to recommend it.

Today's nation is a fairer, more inclusive, more racially tolerant place than the nation of my youth. It is not perfect by any stretch of the imagination, but it is a whole lot better than it used to be.

Opportunity appears everywhere—as long as you have education or skills. People have more choices than ever before, even if it often seems that they are all within a very narrow range. But despite all the problems we see daily, on the news and in the world around us, the new America lets more people exercise their abilities better than did the old.

But one thing we don't do as well as we used to is transmit the meaning of our society and the price it takes to keep all the prerogatives we take for granted. That's what Memorial Day used to be for. It was the day when we remembered the sacrifices individuals made for the collective whole.

Now Memorial Day is a three-day weekend, the semiofficial start of summer. People head to the lake or have a party in the backyard. School is almost out for the kids and everybody is rushing headlong into a summer of fun.

The parades of yesteryear have shrunk, attended by fewer and fewer people, and older and older people, every year. TV news cameras show up, as do politicians galore—especially in an election year. Teary-eyed widows and descendents make good copy and great campaign props, but there is something far less reverential about the entire process than I remember.

This year, I would like to see us do it a little differently. We are in the middle of an increasingly unpopular war, and American families of all kinds have sacrificed and suffered losses because of it. Many have lost loved ones, young men who will never grow older. Even more have had family members away from them for a very long time.

This year especially, we should take heed of Memorial Day, both as a day of remembrance and as one of reflections. Before you hoist another beer, stop and take a minute to reflect on what it requires to preserve the freedoms we all value in this country. With this small gesture, we would do honor to those who have done us the honor of protecting our nation. It may not be much, but it would be a start.

May 28, 2006
Las Vegas Sun

60

A Better Way to Hold Elections

WITH THE PRIMARY ON TUESDAY, the political season is in full swing. Candidates grovel at any altar; they will profess any faith in exchange for votes. They attack opponents with similar views, distort each other's voting records and in some cases lineage, and it seems, will do or say anything to get elected.

Nevada is always an interesting place to follow politics. Where else could you find two people with bankruptcies running for state treasurer? Dead people have won elections in other states. This year a recently deceased candidate has more than a fighting chance to win the Republican primary for state treasurer. And, of course, we have the usual array of carpetbaggers, people with short histories in the state who typically have made money and seek to turn it into political office.

We have our share of eccentrics in state politics. The lieutenant governor's race has Lonnie Hammargren, a former holder of this office, who inexplicably wants it again. Eccentric is generous in his case. Bob Stupak is also running. He needs no introduction to Nevadans. His unusual behavior precedes him.

Don't forget the Second Congressional District, where the Club for Growth is trying to buy the seat for Sharron Angle. She seems unable to raise a dollar except for the club's contribution. Do they think we are so blind that outside money will triumph over experience?

The primary system forces candidates into a bind. In an age when belonging to a political party means less every year, the primary system enshrines party affiliation. Candidates have to appeal to the dwindling party faithful to attain the nomination and then, in the general election, have to tack to the center where most of Nevada's voters reside.

It is very hard to go from the extremes to the middle in just three months. This strategy requires vast expenditures of capital, mostly on TV commercials, with the sole purpose of recasting a candidate as someone who can appeal to the majority of Nevadans. Certainly their primary positions are a liability in the general election.

Could there be a better way? Could we dispense with the primary, acknowledging that party affiliation is a relic and the primaries encourage extreme positions?

There are other states that do this differently. Although I would not hold Louisiana as a model for anything political, its primary system makes more sense than ours.

In the Pelican State, all the candidates are grouped together in the primary. Party makes no difference, nor does any other distinction. If one candidate tops 50 percent of the vote, they win. Simple as that. No general election.

If no one tops 50 percent, the two top vote-getters proceed to a general election. They may be from the same party. They may be from no party at all. But they have proven themselves in an open primary and earned a shot at the run-off.

This makes a lot of sense for us. It would force candidates to be realistic about the offices they seek. This year we have been told that the lieutenant governor of Nevada is an integral player in the struggle over illegal immigration. As specious as that claim is, it has a certain appeal to the primary voters on one side of the aisle. In an open primary, this ridiculous perspective would be exposed as the fraud that it is.

An open primary would also diminish the power of political parties. Candidates would be forced to find the broad center earlier in the process. Such a system might yield more diverse candidates, people who did not have to earn their bona fides in a political party.

There are drawbacks to any system. We would be bombarded and the airwaves would be dripping with political messages even earlier than they do now. If someone won an open primary, we would not have to endure more political commercials.

Money might have an even greater role in politics than it does now. An open primary's biggest drawback is that it could convert fundraising into office. The candidates with the most money early in the game would have the best opportunities to get their message out.

But reviewing the primary system in Nevada is a valuable exercise. The state has changed dramatically, but the political system remains from an earlier Nevada. As Americans alter their political habits, the system needs to change with them. As with any change, we have to make sure it yields the ends that the public desires.

August 13, 2006
Las Vegas Sun

61

Fiscal Divides in America

A COUPLE OF YEARS AGO I pulled up to a building where a large sign welcomed me to "Home Courts," a combination gym that sponsored youth and adult basketball and volleyball leagues and instruction.

The sign advertised courts for rent, leagues for kids and adults, and space for parties. A schedule offered a weekend volleyball tournament, advertising club teams from around the region. As my son and I entered, the sound of squeaking sneakers, dribbling basketballs, and excited young voices was music to my ears. It brought back memories of my own youth, of the endless games that dominated my afternoons and summers.

The gym we entered was large and wonderful, with sixteen courts of various kinds, and basketball hoops that descended from the ceiling to any range of heights. Three games and a volleyball practice were going on. My nine-year-old beamed and ran to join his new team. I stood by the side, awestruck. Wow! What a great place for a kid to play some ball and make some friends.

Then it struck me: This was pay space, not play space; private, not public. There was nothing public about it. You had to belong to get in, and for good reason. The investment had to be enormous. A marketing department encouraged parents to sign their kids up for leagues, and there were no scholarships for needy kids advertised.

This was a business, where someone stood to make a significant profit off the decline in the concept of community and public space that has overtaken America. As much as I liked it, I was also repelled.

Home Courts was a far cry from my youth, when we went to the schoolyard and played against all comers, the winners keeping the court sometimes from early in the morning until it was too dark to see. In those days, there were no adults around, no restrooms except the bushes, no parents wearing jerseys emblazoned with their kids' names, no electronic scoreboard, no sense of hierarchy except that among the kids, and no one to solve the inevitable problems that occurred except the kids who wanted to knock off the nonsense and keep the game going.

Everywhere you look, private space masquerades as public or at least community space. The motto over the waiting area at a local dance studio reads: "This isn't a lobby, it's a neighborhood." Again, the only people there have paid; the only reason to be there is because your child is enrolled in a dance or gymnastics class. So admittance to the neighborhood costs, and is driven by affinity, not the proximity of old.

The world today is different: For the most part, my kids do the same things I did, play the same games in the same ways. The difference is they do so in private space for which we pay; I played in spaces that everyone shared and nobody had to shell out a few bucks to get in.

Here is a metaphor for what has happened to the United States. What we once did in public we now do in private space; what was once free now has an admission charge.

This division is a step on the road to a very different society. Turmoil in the American economy in the 1970s and 1980s broke the middle class into two distinct groups, the large downwardly mobile cohort of the old middle class and the professionals and entrepreneurs who pushed upward.

The 1990s restored prosperity, placing a premium on the trappings of privilege, on the ways people can make themselves distinctive. With immigration at an all-time high and local news featuring mayhem, the association is clear. Americans fear people unlike them. Everyone knows their rights; few understand that they come with obligations. People widely perceive that the protections of the private sector are better than those of the public.

Even I have become comfortable at Home Courts; now, we know everyone there and they're our affinity friends. We socialize casually, transport kids to and fro, and generally keep an eye on what goes on. The life of the young is in view of their parents. We feel safer and maybe they do, too. But if we do, it's because paying for space excludes those who can't, and American society today presumes that if you can't pay for space, there is something wrong with you.

August 27, 2006
Las Vegas Sun

62

Are We Better Off Now

Than We Were in 2001?

IT HAS BEEN FIVE YEARS since the atrocities of 9/11, the cowardly and unprovoked attack on American civilians perpetrated by a group of Islamic fundamentalist terrorists. This was a shocking moment, not only for the moral bankruptcy of the assault but also for the insidious character of the logic behind it. They didn't care who they killed as long as they killed. Then as now, Muslims, the supposed brethren of the attackers, are fair game. It is not a human calculus.

This was not the first such attack on American soil. That infamous distinction belongs to the British, who sacked Washington, D.C., and burned the White House during the War of 1812. There have been other attacks, of course. Pancho Villa invaded Columbus, New Mexico, during the Mexican Revolution. He had financed his revolution by credit extended him by local merchants. When he wanted more weapons and supplies, they turned him down cold. Villa had maxed out his credit. He attacked in response.

Pearl Harbor stands out as the worst until 9/11, and there is no more moving place for me in the United States. I felt obligated to read every name on the wall, fighting back tears all the while. But then, I have not yet been to Ground Zero.

September 11 was different in that civilians were the primary target. More like the Oklahoma City bombing than any previous attack on our soil, 9/11 did more than prove that oceans no longer shielded us from the happenings in the rest of the world. It at long last punctured our age-old insularity.

Five years is a long time and Americans deserve a reckoning. What have we accomplished since 9/11 and where has it gotten us? Are we better off, as Ronald Reagan used to ask, than we were in August 2001?

The elephant in the West Wing is obvious. Where is Osama? We have spent billions of dollars we don't have and this SOB is still running loose, thumbing his nose at us. I want him a lot worse than I ever did Saddam Hussein. The world is not that big and nobody is that elusive.

September 11 simultaneously made George W. Bush and brought him back to cold reality. Before 9/11, he was the accidental president, a lackluster leader whose administration had little direction or purpose. In the aftermath of the atrocities of that fateful day, he morphed into a leader. With the support of the world, we were poised to remake political culture for a new age. Even the Middle East seemed within reach.

But the man didn't have the gravitas. He wasn't all he had appeared to be when he stood at the smoking, gaping hole and inspired a stunned and grieving nation. From the "Mission Accomplished" stunt to his concerted assault on the rights we all hold sacred, he has shown neither style nor substance.

So instead of a safer world, we have more chaos and many fewer ways to find solutions. We have ignored the wisest piece of political advice ever uttered—keep your friends close and your enemies closer. We can't even talk directly to our adversaries.

Worse, our allies now fear us and don't trust our motives. When we say that we want to seed democracy across the globe, they look askance and wonder what our real objective is. Now we are virtually alone and friendless, with a growing reputation as the neighborhood bully.

And then there is the quagmire of Iraq. Things are clearly not getting better and we have been there more than three years. We have not changed the face of the Middle East. It seems even more unlikely that such a goal was ever possible.

It is often said that people get the government they deserve. Our apathy has let our leaders get us into this quandary. Most of us have not paid attention as decisions that are crucial to our future as individuals and as a nation were implemented. We have been deceived on a number of occasions, but the obligation still falls on the citizenry to be vigilant. We have not been so and the fault is ours.

Five years have passed. The world is neither safer nor better. When we remember that horrid day, we must think about where we will be on the tenth anniversary of 9/11. By then, if the American public demands it, we might have a clear charter to a better world. Let us all aim higher.

September 10, 2006
Las Vegas Sun

63

The Positive, Social Value

of Eminent Domain

BACK IN THE AGE OF VINYL, I had an idea. Records—remember them?—sold for about four dollars new and I had amassed quite a collection. I had about $500 and I was pretty sure there were others as fanatical about music as me. I decided to open a used record store.

I figured if I could buy enough for a buck, I could sell them for two dollars apiece. I could not only make a little money, but I also would no longer have to pay for my own music. All that remained was to find a place close enough to the local university to capitalize on the fickle tastes of college students.

It turned out a local landlord would lease me exactly what I needed, about 150 square feet across the street from the psychology building and near the bar district. A head shop, one of those hangovers from the 1960s, a used clothing store, and a low-end steakhouse rounded out the block. I balked at the three-year lease, but when I realized he couldn't get blood from a stone if I defaulted, I signed the deal.

Eighteen months later, I had a minor hit on my hands. The concept worked and I was making money, getting all the music I had ever dreamed of for free, and there was a bonus I hadn't even considered: girls now knew who I was. I decided to branch out into comic books and paperbacks. I began to see a career in what started out as a way to cut the cost of my favorite pastime.

Then the shoe dropped. The only reason I could afford the location was that the university had been negotiating to buy it and by keeping his ragtag bunch of properties filled, the landlord thought he improved his leverage. It didn't matter one whit. The university tired of his exorbitant demands and with legislative funding for a new speech and hearing building in hand, the state initiated condemnation proceedings under the eminent domain statute. The first I knew of the entire process was when the eviction notice hit my hands.

For the first time in my life, I went to see a lawyer. I thought I was in a great position. I had almost half my lease yet to run and I had signed a document that bound both parties and was enforceable in court. He looked at me with tired gray eyes and said, "Young man, let me teach you a little something about American law."

The university had all the cards, including the ace of trump. My lease was not worth the paper it was printed on. I received $3,000 to move my business to another location. Of course, I could not find one that I could afford. So much for my dreams of empire. For many years, I stewed about the injustice I thought had been done to me.

A few years ago I returned to my hometown for a high school reunion. I went by the corner where my store once stood and found a five-story brick building, beautifully designed, with a sign that announced "Speech and Hearing Research Center." The structure was home to some of the most important work in cochlear implants and speech therapy. Research there brought in millions and created jobs galore. I finally had to admit that the university's use had greater social value than my little record store.

Eminent domain is always controversial, for it involves taking private property for public use. It is an essential tool for government precisely because it can be used to circumvent people like my old landlord, who sought to exploit the state's need for his location. In the end, the public interest was better served by the speech and hearing center and the greedy owner did not unduly enrich himself at the public trough.

As Nevada struggles with the ballot question PISTOL (The Peoples' Initiative to Stop Taking of Our Land), the effort to limit the state's power to use eminent domain, the question is obviously messier than proponents and much of the news coverage would have you think.

There is no faster way to increase government expenditures in a rapidly growing state than to give landowners a license to raid public coffers. PISTOL demands consideration of the long-term implications for the public. We need to know what our dance with unrestricted property rights will cost before we vote it up or down.

September 17, 2006
Las Vegas Sun

64

Underhanded Tactics by the NEI

THE NUCLEAR ENERGY INSTITUTE is at it again. Nevada should pass a law declaring the NEI a terrorist entity, much as the U.S. government does with Islamic organizations, for its latest attempt to thwart the will of the citizenry with an end run to place hazardous waste in the Silver State without consulting us.

Make no mistake. This insidious bunch is trying to push its camel nose underneath our tent and I guarantee that they hope you are distracted. It is dirty pool, no doubt.

Just before the election, when a nongovernmental lobbying entity like the NEI can be assured its generosity to incumbents in both parties will diminish any congressional resistance to its shenanigans, they are floating a bill that would permit the temporary storage of nuclear waste in Nevada.

The Nuclear Energy Institute has to date been ineffectual. Sure it bought a few of our lamest politicians and an occasional newsman in an effort to sway public opinion. These efforts failed, testimony to the good sense of Nevada's people.

A few months ago, I declared that our persistent opposition to Yucca Mountain had finally helped to turn the corner in the battle against that project. At the same time, I cautioned that we would see many attempts to sneak nuclear waste into the state. Some efforts would be aboveground; others would be downright deceitful.

This one is despicable. It attempts to buy the state for a paltry $25 million a year, essentially for giving up our sovereignty and integrity. That is roughly twenty dollars for every man, woman, and child in Nevada.

Let us briefly review. In the fiscal year ending June 2006, Nevada collected a little more than $1 billion in sales tax. The gaming tax netted another $838 million. That is about two-thirds of the state's revenue. We are no penny ante operation these days.

Even if we were inclined to pursue such a solution, the offer is insulting. It is warm spit in the face of the state, a fundamental miscalculation that will serve to stiffen our resolve to defeat this beast. They are not only trying to go around us, but they are also trying to do it on the cheap.

So much for the argument that we should negotiate for benefits. It is now clear that negotiations would be fruitless. As anyone in Las Vegas well knows, a lowball offer out of the gate is a signal of a lack of respect. I don't know about you, but I never deal with people who don't respect my point of view.

Until I moved to Nevada some fifteen years ago, I had little sympathy for states' rights arguments. I saw states' rights as a backward-looking philosophy, one that carried the baggage of the South in the Civil War and, even worse, was laden with the stench of the opposition to civil rights.

My time in the Silver State has softened my view. The egregious conduct of the federal government in Nevada, first with aboveground nuclear testing, then with the travesty of the "Screw Nevada" bill in 1987 that authorized Yucca Mountain, and finally with the deceitful and likely illegal running of the project, it has become hard to defend national power against that of the state.

Congress has a pretty firm rule: you don't put anything in somebody else's state without checking with them. It is more than courtesy. That means they don't do the same to you.

I don't recall anyone from the Nuclear Energy Institute ever asking us what we thought about interim storage. I deeply resent their conduct in this case, for it is not only underhanded but also offensive. This is an effort to make Nevada the nation's dump through the back door.

A few years ago, I participated in a conference about nuclear waste.

I have the habit of referring to Yucca Mountain as a "dump." One of the other presenters chastised me. He said it was a repository. I countered that it was a dump, a really expensive one, but a dump nonetheless.

The Nuclear Energy Institute could do well to remember my little exchange. No end runs and no back-door entry. A state must have the power to control its destiny, especially in the case of a craven assault by a lobbying group.

October 1, 2006
Las Vegas Sun

65

Returning Democracy to the People

I AM A POLITICAL JUNKIE from a long line of political junkies, but this campaign season has really turned my stomach. If I hear the phrase "outside of the mainstream" or "out of touch with Nevada" one more time, I may run for office myself.

As Billy Joel once sang in another context, "All it takes are looks and a whole lot of money." I of course have neither, but if I sold my soul to cash-heavy special interests, I too could be viable. Such is the sad state of Nevada and ultimately national politics.

Is there not a candidate out there with a record to run on? Doesn't anyone want to talk about their accomplishments? All I hear, day in and day out, are half-witted appeals to the lowest common denominator, attempts to tar opponents with a broad brush that paints them into a corner. I expect better from people who want to lead the state or represent us in Washington.

It seems the only people who are willing to run on their record are those with a weak opposition. This is what democracy has become, a contest between different piles of money competing for television time. Issues be damned! We are only going to talk about what might have been, not what should be.

There are issues that matter this year. The state of Nevada's schools, immigration, the health care system, the war in Iraq, the question of whether we can trust our leaders, and, of course, growth, all loom large, but they are far from the discourse.

What if we set the bar higher? What if Nevada became the first state in the union to put a cap on political spending? What if we put limits not only on how much a candidate could spend, but also on how that money could be raised?

Imagine this. We could fix the governor's race at $1 million and all the statewide elective offices would follow on a downward sliding scale. The statewide offices would get more than local offices, for people who have to campaign throughout the enormous breadth of the state would need more than those with more limited areas to cover.

We would know a great deal more about our candidates than we do now. On a fixed budget, candidates would have to be money managers. We would also know a great deal more about their priorities, for we would not see the overflowing war chests that we do today. Candidates would have to decide what they wanted us to know and they would have to be efficient in spreading their messages.

They would also have to avail themselves of opportunities to reach the public that they did not have to pay for. This would mean more direct contact with the public, more candidates' forums and debates, more stump speeches and barbecues.

Aspiring officeholders would have to work much harder than they do now, and the work would mean much more. Serious candidates would know their constituents well. We would also be on closer terms with them. We might even return to the first-name basis that long characterized Nevada politics.

Even more, we could put strict limits on how candidates could receive money. Instead of allowing affiliated groups to sully our politics, we could simply bar all private money and create a mechanism that funds our politics. We could get all private money out of politics and level the playing field. Maybe we could lay off the cost on visitors like we do so many other things in the Silver State.

Democracy started in town-size environments and it still works best in intimate settings. Nevada is still small enough that we can have grassroots democracy.

We could remove the acrid stink of special interest money from our politics and turn back the clock to a time when people of differing political persuasions actually talked to each other. Who knows? It might work. One person, one vote. It was always a good idea.

October 29, 2006
Las Vegas Sun

66

Disneyland's Lesson

ON ONE OF THE BUSIEST DAYS of the year, two days after Christmas 2000, I took my family into Disneyland. The place was jammed; it felt more like walking up to a college football bowl game than visiting an amusement park, except that an enormous percentage of the people were small. They stopped selling tickets that morning at about 10:30 when the park reached its capacity of a hundred and five thousand. The happiest place on earth was busting at the seams and was a little too full to be all that happy.

With an exhausted five-year-old in tow, I ducked out of the mayhem in search of something else to do. Near Main Street, the entrance to the park, I spotted something that had always caught my eye but that I'd never stopped to see before. "Great Moments with Mr. Lincoln," a testimony to Walt Disney's idea of democracy, had been a fixture of the park, the closest thing to a heritage attraction there, but it was not terribly popular with most of the Disneyland visitors, more anxious to fastpass Indiana Jones than learn even popularized history. We entered a museumlike interior—my five-year-old said with exasperation, "Dad, this is just a museum"—with a replica of the capitol. It felt sterile, vacant, devoid of inspiration of any kind. We were in for a short stay out of the mayhem.

At the last second I noticed a large well-appointed theater. Three hundred red plush seats sat almost empty, with a smattering of older white people. The room was cool and comfortable and we settled in to watch. The lights dimmed and began a tribute to the ideals and ideas of democracy that accompanied a hagiography of Abraham Lincoln right out of the 1950s. The music was triumphalist, reminiscent of 1962's *How the West was Won*, one of the great epics of American expansion; the sentiments were lofty, and the canonization of Lincoln complete. The voiceover quoted Lincoln from the Lincoln-Douglas debates, described the turmoil of the Civil War, and conveniently skipped the assassination. It was stirring, mindful of the ideals of democracy and the high sentiments that used to accompany public rhetoric in the United States.

Then the curtain rose and a robotic Abraham Lincoln appeared, seated in a chair designed to recall the Lincoln Memorial. He rose and spoke, bits and pieces that both continued the lofty ideals of the voiceover and added the personal dimension, the pain of power and hard decisions, the importance Lincoln placed on being morally right, and the conflicts that raged inside him. "Dad, that's a robot," my five-year-old said and the ideas were well over his head. But it had the feel, the meaning, the power of the past, robot or not, and it offered an appreciation for American democratic idealism that, while dated and arguably exclusionist, communicated strongly much more than entertainment. Even the sign on the wall as we departed that equated free enterprise with free people was not enough to diminish the powerful patriotism that infused this production.

But on the busiest day of the year, few stopped to see Mr. Lincoln. They rushed onward, to wait in interminably long lines to ride the fake Matterhorn or to spin in the dark in Space Mountain. Thunder Mountain Railroad, "the wildest ride in the wilderness," the hackneyed voiceover proclaimed, held more appeal than American history and the hard choices of a freedom-loving leader. Here was a lesson about cultural tourism, about its reach in postmodern, postindustrial society. On a day when easily half the people in Disneyland spoke Spanish and Spanish-speaking children outnumbered all others by a factor of four, the principle ideal of democracy had little meaning. Culture truly has become liberal consumerism, what we share with people from all places. The right to choose our goods has become more important than the right to choose our friends.

—Unpublished

INDEX